W9-BXT-814

DEMCO

COMPLETE GUIDE TO HOME CANNING AND PRESERVING

Second Revised Edition

U. S. Department of Agriculture

DOVER PUBLICATIONS, INC.
Mineola, New York

Publisher's Note

This book was originally published as a consumer service of the United States Department of Agriculture. Each of the seven guides that made up the original book was numbered separately. Although the pages have been renumbered consecutively, the page numbers of the original publication have also been retained in parentheses in order to permit the use of the original tables of contents, indexes and textual cross-references.

Bibliographical Note

Complete Guide to Home Canning and Preserving (Second Revised Edition), first published by Dover Publications, Inc., in 1999 (earlier editions 1973 and 1994), is an unabridged reprint of Agriculture Information Bulletin No. 539, *Complete Guide to Home Canning,* September 1994. The color illustrations in the original have been converted to black-and-white in the Dover edition.

Library of Congress Cataloging-in-Publication Data

United States. Dept. of Agriculture.
    Complete guide to home canning and preserving / U.S. Department of Agriculture. — 2nd rev. ed.
        p.   cm.
    ISBN 0-486-40931-7 (pbk.)
    1. Canning and preserving.   I. Title.
TX601.U63   1999
641.4'2—dc21   99-16803
                                                                                        CIP

Manufactured in the United States of America
Dover Publications, Inc., 31 East 2nd Street, Mineola, N.Y. 11501

Acknowledgments

The creation of an Extension Service Center for Excellence at the Penn State University made it possible to conduct the research necessary to revise four previously published bulletins for canning foods in the home. The Center, no longer in operation, was a cooperative effort of the Extension Service, Cooperative State Research Service, and the Penn State University with Gerald D. Kuhn, Ph.D., of the Penn State University as Director.

The Extension Service wishes to credit the primary development of this guide to Gerald D. Kuhn, Elizabeth L. Andress (currently with the University of Georgia), and Thomas S. Dimick. Extension staff who assisted in preparing this guide include Milton P. Baldauf, Catherine E. Adams, Nancy T. Sowers, and Vincent G. Hughes. Extension staff who assisted in this revision include Kenneth N. Hall (University of Connecticut) and Thomas W. Poore. Research for the smoked fish recommendation was conducted by Carolyn Raab and Ken Hilderbrand (Oregon State University) with partial funding from the OSU Extension Sea Grant Program. All have contributed significant ideas and time in making this guide a truly up-to-date research-based publication.

Complete Guide to Home Canning

Caution: To prevent the risk of botulism, low-acid and tomato foods not canned according to the recommendations in this publication or according to other USDA-endorsed recommendations should be boiled even if you detect no signs of spoilage. At altitudes below 1,000 ft, boil foods for 10 minutes. Add an additional minute of boiling time for each additional 1,000 ft elevation.

Reference to commercial products and services is made with the understanding that no discrimination is intended and no endorsement by the U.S. Department of Agriculture is implied. Clear Jel® is mentioned because it is the only suitable product that is presently available to the general public through distributors of specialty products.

Preface

Home canning has changed greatly in the 170 years since it was introduced as a way to preserve food. Scientists have found ways to produce safer, higher quality products. The first part of this publication explains the scientific principles on which canning techniques are based, discusses canning equipment, and describes the proper use of jars and lids. It describes basic canning ingredients and procedures and how to use them to achieve safe, high-quality canned products. Finally, it helps you decide whether or not and how much to can.

The second part of this publication is a series of canning guides for specific foods. These guides offer detailed directions for making sugar syrups; and for canning fruits and fruit products, tomatoes and tomato products, vegetables, red meats, poultry, seafoods, and pickles and relishes. Handy guidelines for choosing the right quantities and quality of raw foods accompany each set of directions for fruits, tomatoes, and vegetables. Most recipes are designed to yield a full canner load of pints or quarts. Finally, processing adjustments for altitudes above sea level are given for each food.

This publication contains many new research-based recommendations for canning safer and better quality food at home. It is an invaluable resource book for persons who are canning food for the first time. Experienced canners will find updated information to help them improve their canning practices.

For Safety's Sake

Pressure canning is the only recommended method for canning meat, poultry, seafood, and vegetables. The bacterium *Clostridium botulinum* is destroyed in low-acid foods when they are processed at the correct time and pressure in pressure canners. Using boiling water canners for these foods poses a real risk of botulism poisoning.

If *Clostridium botulinum* bacteria survive and grow inside a sealed jar of food, they can produce a poisonous toxin. Even a taste of food containing this toxin can be fatal. Boiling food 10 minutes at altitudes below 1,000 ft destroys this poison when it is present. For altitudes at and above 1,000 ft, add 1 additional minute per 1,000 ft additional elevation. Caution: To prevent the risk of botulism, low-acid and tomato foods not canned according to the recommendations in this publication or according to other USDA-endorsed recommendations should be boiled as above, even if you detect no signs of spoilage. All low-acid foods canned according to the approved recommendations may be eaten without boiling them when you are sure of all the following:
- Food was processed in a pressure canner.
- Gauge of the pressure canner was accurate.
- Up-to-date researched process times and pressures were used for the size of jar, style of pack, and kind of food being canned.
- The process time and pressure recommended for sterilizing the food at your altitude was followed.
- Jar lid is firmly sealed and concave.
- Nothing has leaked from jar.
- No liquid spurts out when jar is opened.
- No unnatural or "off" odors can be detected.

Do Your Canned Foods Pass This Test?

Overall appearance
- Good proportion of solid to liquid
- Full pack with proper headspace
- Liquid just covering solid
- Free of air bubbles
- Free of imperfections—stems, cores, seeds
- Good seals
- Practical pack that is done quickly and easily

Fruit and vegetables
- Pieces uniform in size and shape
- Characteristic, uniform color
- Shape retained—not broken or mushy
- Proper maturity

Liquid or syrup
- Clear and free from sediment

Determining Your Altitude Above Sea Level

It is important to know your approximate elevation or altitude above sea level in order to determine a safe processing time for canned foods. Since the boiling temperature of liquid is lower at higher elevations, it is critical that additional time be given for the safe processing of foods at altitudes above sea level.

It is not practical to include a list of altitudes in this guide, since there is wide variation within a State and even a county. For example, the State of Kansas has areas with altitudes varying between 75 ft to 4,039 ft above sea level. Kansas is not generally thought to have high altitudes, but there are many areas of the State where adjustments for altitude must be considered. Colorado, on the other hand, has people living in areas between 3,000 and 10,000 ft above sea level. They tend to be more conscious of the need to make altitude adjustments in the various processing schedules. To list altitudes for specific counties may actually be misleading, due to the differences in geographic terrain within a county.

If you are unsure about the altitude where you will be canning foods, consult your county Extension agent. An alternative source of information would be your local district conservationist with the Soil Conservation Service.

CONTENTS

A detailed table of contents will be found at the beginning of each section.

CONVERSION TABLES FOR FOREIGN EQUIVALENTS

DRY INGREDIENTS

Ounces	Grams	Grams	Ounces	Pounds	Kilograms	Kilograms	Pounds
1 =	28.35	1 =	0.035	1 =	0.454	1 =	2.205
2	56.70	2	0.07	2	0.91	2	4.41
3	85.05	3	0.11	3	1.36	3	6.61
4	113.40	4	0.14	4	1.81	4	8.82
5	141.75	5	0.18	5	2.27	5	11.02
6	170.10	6	0.21	6	2.72	6	13.23
7	198.45	7	0.25	7	3.18	7	15.43
8	226.80	8	0.28	8	3.63	8	17.64
9	255.15	9	0.32	9	4.08	9	19.84
10	283.50	10	0.35	10	4.54	10	22.05
11	311.85	11	0.39	11	4.99	11	24.26
12	340.20	12	0.42	12	5.44	12	26.46
13	368.55	13	0.46	13	5.90	13	28.67
14	396.90	14	0.49	14	6.35	14	30.87
15	425.25	15	0.53	15	6.81	15	33.08
16	453.60	16	0.57				

LIQUID INGREDIENTS

Liquid Ounces	Milliliters	Milliliters	Liquid Ounces	Quarts	Liters	Liters	Quarts
1 =	29.573	1 =	0.034	1 =	0.946	1 =	1.057
2	59.15	2	0.07	2	1.89	2	2.11
3	88.72	3	0.10	3	2.84	3	3.17
4	118.30	4	0.14	4	3.79	4	4.23
5	147.87	5	0.17	5	4.73	5	5.28
6	177.44	6	0.20	6	5.68	6	6.34
7	207.02	7	0.24	7	6.62	7	7.40
8	236.59	8	0.27	8	7.57	8	8.45
9	266.16	9	0.30	9	8.52	9	9.51
10	295.73	10	0.33	10	9.47	10	10.57

Gallons (American)	Liters	Liters	Gallons (American)
1 =	3.785	1 =	0.264
2	7.57	2	0.53
3	11.36	3	0.79
4	15.14	4	1.06
5	18.93	5	1.32
6	22.71	6	1.59
7	26.50	7	1.85
8	30.28	8	2.11
9	34.07	9	2.38
10	37.86	10	2.74

Complete Guide to Home Canning, Guide 1

PRINCIPLES OF HOME CANNING

Guide 1

Principles of Home Canning

Table of Contents, Guide 1

Principles of Home Canning

Section	Page

Why can foods?

Canning can be a safe and economical way to preserve quality food at home. Disregarding the value of your labor, canning homegrown food may save you half the cost of buying commercially canned food. Canning favorite and special products to be enjoyed by family and friends is a fulfilling experience and a source of pride for many people.

Many vegetables begin losing some of their vitamins when harvested. Nearly half the vitamins may be lost within a few days unless the fresh produce is cooled or preserved. Within 1 to 2 weeks, even refrigerated produce loses half or more of some of its vitamins. The heating process during canning destroys from one-third to one-half of vitamins A and C, thiamin, and riboflavin. Once canned, additional losses of these sensitive vitamins are from 5 to 20 percent each year. The amounts of other vitamins, however, are only slightly lower in canned compared with fresh food. If vegetables are handled properly and canned promptly after harvest, they can be more nutritious than fresh produce sold in local stores.

The advantages of home canning are lost when you start with poor quality fresh foods; when jars fail to seal properly; when food spoils; and when flavors, texture, color, and nutrients deteriorate during prolonged storage.

The information and guides that follow explain many of these problems and recommend ways to minimize them.

How canning preserves foods

The high percentage of water in most fresh foods makes them very perishable. They spoil or lose their quality for several reasons:
- growth of undesirable microorganisms—bacteria, molds, and yeasts,
- activity of food enzymes,
- reactions with oxygen,
- moisture loss.

Microorganisms live and multiply quickly on the surfaces of fresh food and on the inside of bruised, insect-damaged, and diseased food. Oxygen and enzymes are present throughout fresh food tissues.

Proper canning practices include:
- carefully selecting and washing fresh food,
- peeling some fresh foods,
- hot packing many foods,
- adding acids (lemon juice or vinegar) to some foods,
- using acceptable jars and self-sealing lids,
- processing jars in a boiling-water or pressure canner for the correct period of time.

Collectively, these practices remove oxygen; destroy enzymes; prevent the growth of undesirable bacteria, yeasts, and molds; and help form a high vacuum in jars. Good vacuums form tight seals which keep liquid in and air and microorganisms out.

Ensuring safe canned foods

Growth of the bacterium *Clostridium botulinum* in canned food may cause botulism—a deadly form of food poisoning. These bacteria exist either as spores or as vegetative cells. The spores, which are comparable to plant seeds, can survive harmlessly in soil and water for many years. When ideal conditions exist for growth, the spores produce vegetative cells which multiply rapidly and may produce a deadly toxin within 3 to 4 days of growth in an environment consisting of:
• a moist, low-acid food
• a temperature between 40° and 120°F
• less than 2 percent oxygen
Botulinum spores are on most fresh food surfaces. Because they grow only in the absence of air, they are harmless on fresh foods.

Most bacteria, yeasts, and molds are difficult to remove from food surfaces. Washing fresh food reduces their numbers only slightly. Peeling root crops, underground stem crops, and tomatoes reduces their numbers greatly. Blanching also helps, but the vital controls are the method of canning and making sure the recommended research-based process times, found in these guides, are used.

The processing times in these guides ensure destruction of the largest expected number of heat-resistant microorganisms in home-canned foods. Properly sterilized canned food will be free of spoilage if lids seal and jars are stored below 95°F. Storing jars at 50° to 70°F enhances retention of quality.

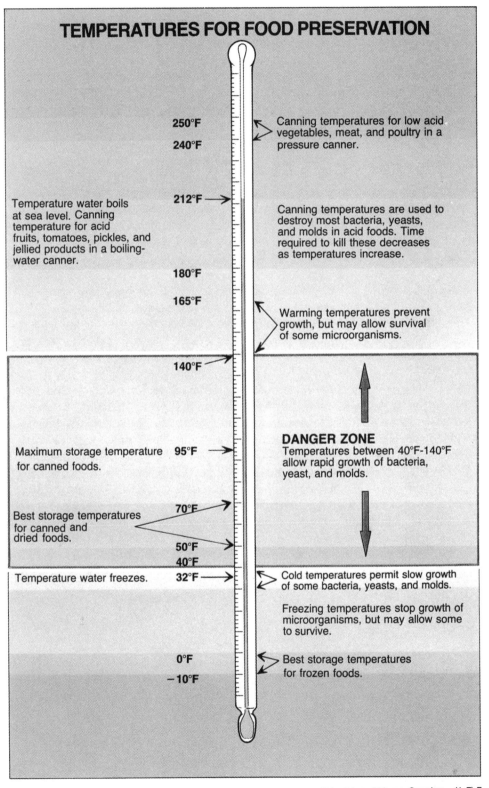

TEMPERATURES FOR FOOD PRESERVATION

250°F
240°F
Canning temperatures for low acid vegetables, meat, and poultry in a pressure canner.

Temperature water boils at sea level. Canning temperature for acid fruits, tomatoes, pickles, and jellied products in a boiling-water canner.
212°F
Canning temperatures are used to destroy most bacteria, yeasts, and molds in acid foods. Time required to kill these decreases as temperatures increase.

180°F
165°F
Warming temperatures prevent growth, but may allow survival of some microorganisms.

140°F

DANGER ZONE
Temperatures between 40°F-140°F allow rapid growth of bacteria, yeast, and molds.

Maximum storage temperature for canned foods. **95°F**

Best storage temperatures for canned and dried foods. **70°F**
50°F
40°F

Temperature water freezes. **32°F**
Cold temperatures permit slow growth of some bacteria, yeasts, and molds.

Freezing temperatures stop growth of microorganisms, but may allow some to survive.

0°F
−10°F
Best storage temperatures for frozen foods.

Food acidity and processing methods

Whether food should be processed in a pressure canner or boiling-water canner to control botulinum bacteria depends on the acidity in the food. Acidity may be natural, as in most fruits, or added, as in pickled food. *Low-acid* canned foods contain too little acidity to prevent the growth of these bacteria. *Acid* foods contain enough acidity to block their growth, or destroy them more rapidly when heated. The term "pH" is a measure of acidity; the lower its value, the more acid the food. The acidity level in foods can be increased by adding lemon juice, citric acid, or vinegar.

Low-acid foods have pH values higher than 4.6. They include red meats, seafood, poultry, milk, and all fresh vegetables except for most tomatoes. Most mixtures of low-acid and acid foods also have pH values above 4.6 unless their recipes include enough lemon juice, citric acid, or vinegar to make them acid foods. Acid foods have a pH of 4.6 or lower. They include fruits, pickles, sauerkraut, jams, jellies, marmalades, and fruit butters.

Although tomatoes usually are considered an acid food, some are now known to have pH values slightly above 4.6. Figs also have pH values slightly above 4.6. Therefore, if they are to be canned as acid foods, these products must be acidified to a pH of 4.6 or lower with lemon juice or citric acid. Properly acidified tomatoes and figs are acid foods and can be safely processed in a boiling-water canner.

Botulinum spores are very hard to destroy at boiling-water temperatures; the higher the canner temperature, the more easily they are destroyed. Therefore, all low-acid foods should be sterilized at temperatures of 240° to 250°F, attainable with pressure canners operated at 10 to 15 PSIG. PSIG means pounds per square inch of pressure as measured by gauge. The more familiar "PSI" designation is used hereafter in this publication. At temperatures of 240° to 250°F, the time needed to destroy bacteria in low-acid canned food ranges from 20 to 100 minutes. The exact time depends on the kind of food being canned, the way it is packed into jars, and the size of jars. The time needed to safely process low-acid foods in a boiling-water canner ranges from 7 to 11 hours; the time needed to process acid foods in boiling water varies from 5 to 85 minutes.

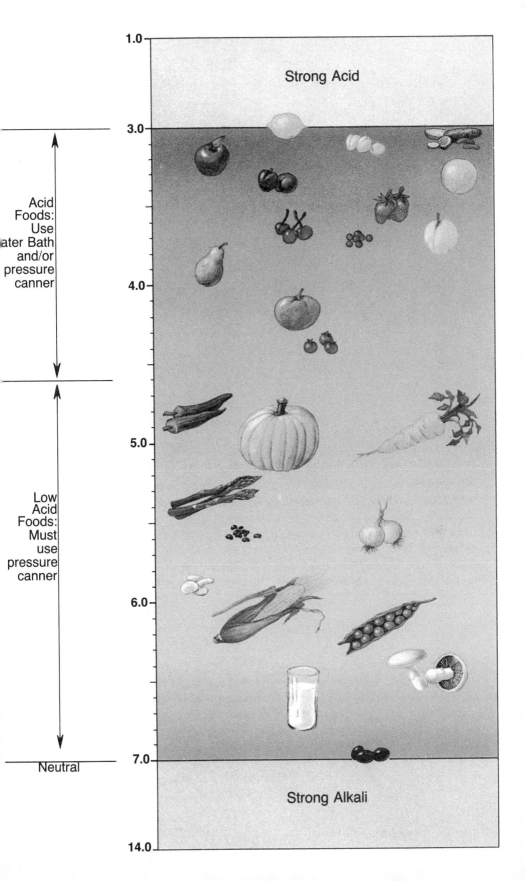

10,000 ft = 194°F

8,000 ft = 197°F

6,000 ft = 201°F

4,000 ft = 204°F

2,000 ft = 208°F

Sea level = 212°F

Process adjustments at high altitudes

Using the process time for canning food at sea level may result in spoilage if you live at altitudes of 1,000 feet or more. Water boils at lower temperatures as altitude increases. Lower boiling temperatures are less effective for killing bacteria. Increasing the process time or canner pressure compensates for lower boiling temperatures. Therefore, when you use the guides, select the proper processing time or canner pressure for the altitude where you live. If you do not know the altitude, contact your local county Extension agent. An alternative source of information would be the local district conservationist with the Soil Conservation Service.

Equipment and methods not recommended

Open-kettle canning and the processing of freshly filled jars in conventional ovens, microwave ovens, and dishwashers are not recommended, because these practices do not prevent all risks of spoilage. Steam canners are not recommended because processing times for use with current models have not been adequately researched. Because steam canners do not heat foods in the same manner as boiling-water canners, their use with boiling-water process times may result in spoilage. It is not recommended that pressure processes in excess of 15 PSI be applied when using new pressure canning equipment. So-called canning powders are useless as preservatives and do not replace the need for proper heat processing. Jars with wire bails and glass caps make attractive antiques or storage containers for dry food ingredients but are not recommended for use in canning. One-piece zinc porcelain-lined caps are also no longer recommended. Both glass and zinc caps use flat rubber rings for sealing jars, but too often fail to seal properly.

Ensuring high-quality canned foods

Begin with good-quality fresh foods suitable for canning. Quality varies among varieties of fruits and vegetables. Many county Extension offices can recommend varieties best suited for canning. Examine food carefully for freshness and wholesomeness. Discard diseased and moldy food. Trim small diseased lesions or spots from food.

Can fruits and vegetables picked from your garden or purchased from nearby producers when the products are at their peak of quality—within 6 to 12 hours after harvest for most vegetables. For best quality, apricots, nectarines, peaches, pears, and plums should be ripened 1 or more days between harvest and canning. If you must delay the canning of other fresh produce, keep it in a shady, cool place.

Fresh home-slaughtered red meats and poultry should be chilled and canned without delay. Do not can meat from sickly or diseased animals. Ice fish and seafoods after harvest, eviscerate immediately, and can them within 2 days.

Maintaining color and flavor in canned food

To maintain good natural color and flavor in stored canned food, you must:
• Remove oxygen from food tissues and jars,
• Quickly destroy the food enzymes,
• Obtain high jar vacuums and airtight jar seals.

Follow these guidelines to ensure that your canned foods retain optimum colors and flavors during processing and storage:
• Use only high-quality foods which are at the proper maturity and are free of diseases and bruises.
• Use the hot-pack method, especially with acid foods to be processed in boiling water.
• Don't unnecessarily expose prepared foods to air. Can them as soon as possible.
• While preparing a canner load of jars, keep peeled, halved, quartered, sliced, or diced apples, apricots, nectarines, peaches, and pears in a solution of 3 grams (3,000 milligrams) ascorbic acid to 1 gallon of cold water. This procedure is also useful in maintaining the natural color of mushrooms and potatoes, and for preventing stem-end discoloration in cherries and grapes. You can get ascorbic acid in several forms:

Pure powdered form—seasonally available among canners' supplies in supermarkets. One level teaspoon of pure powder weighs about 3 grams. Use 1 teaspoon per gallon of water as a treatment solution.

Vitamin C tablets—economical and available year-round in many stores. Buy 500-milligram tablets; crush and dissolve six tablets per gallon of water as a treatment solution.

Commercially prepared mixes of ascorbic and citric acid—seasonally available among canners' supplies in supermarkets. Sometimes citric acid powder is sold in supermarkets, but it is less effective in controlling discoloration. If you choose to use these products, follow the manufacturer's directions.

- Fill hot foods into jars and adjust headspace as specified in recipes.
- Tighten screw bands securely, but if you are especially strong, not as tightly as possible.
- Process and cool jars.
- Store the jars in a relatively cool, dark place, preferably between 50° and 70°F.
- Can no more food than you will use within a year.

Advantages of hot-packing

Many fresh foods contain from 10 percent to more than 30 percent air. How long canned food retains high quality depends on how much air is removed from food before jars are sealed.

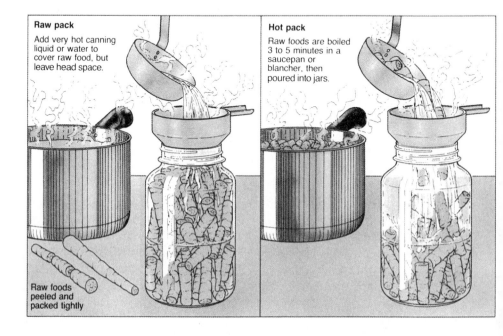

Raw pack
Add very hot canning liquid or water to cover raw food, but leave head space.

Raw foods peeled and packed tightly

Hot pack
Raw foods are boiled 3 to 5 minutes in a saucepan or blancher, then poured into jars.

Raw-packing is the practice of filling jars tightly with freshly prepared, but unheated food. Such foods, especially fruit, will float in the jars. The entrapped air in and around the food may cause discoloration within 2 to 3 months of storage. Raw-packing is more suitable for vegetables processed in a pressure canner.

Hot-packing is the practice of heating freshly prepared food to boiling, simmering it 2 to 5 minutes, and promptly filling jars loosely with the boiled food. Whether food has been hot-packed or raw-packed, the juice, syrup, or water to be added to the foods should also be heated to boiling before adding it to the jars. This practice helps to remove air from food tissues, shrinks food, helps keep the food from floating in the jars, increases vacuum in sealed jars, and improves shelf life. Preshrinking food permits filling more food into each jar.

Hot-packing is the best way to remove air and is the preferred pack style for foods processed in a boiling-water canner. At first, the color of hot-packed foods may appear no better than that of raw-packed foods, but within a short storage period, both color and flavor of hot-packed foods will be superior.

Controlling headspace

The unfilled space above the food in a jar and below its lid is termed headspace. Directions for canning specify leaving 1/4-inch for jams and jellies, 1/2-inch for fruits and tomatoes to be processed in boiling water, and from 1- to 1-1/4-inches in low-acid foods to be processed in a pressure canner. This space is needed for expansion of food as jars are processed, and for forming vacuums in cooled jars. The extent of expansion is determined by the air content in the food and by the processing temperature. Air expands greatly when heated to high temperatures; the higher the temperature, the greater the expansion. Foods expand less than air when heated.

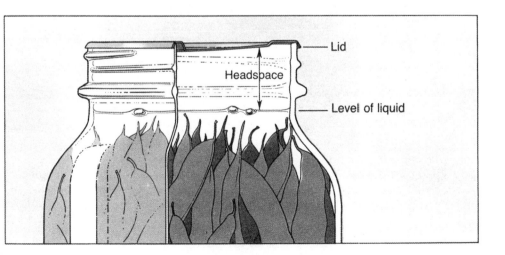

Lid

Headspace

Level of liquid

Jars and lids

Food may be canned in glass jars or metal containers. Metal containers can be used only once. They require special sealing equipment and are much more costly than jars.

Regular and wide-mouth Mason-type, threaded, home-canning jars with self-sealing lids are the best choice. They are available in 1/2 pint, pint, 1-1/2 pint, quart, and 1/2 gallon sizes. The standard jar mouth opening is about 2-3/8 inches. Wide-mouth jars have openings of about 3 inches, making them more easily filled and emptied. Half-gallon jars may be used for canning very acid juices. Regular-mouth decorator jelly jars are available in 8 and 12 ounce sizes. With careful use and handling, Mason jars may be reused many times, requiring only new lids each time. When jars and lids are used properly, jar seals and vacuums are excellent and jar breakage is rare.

Most commercial pint- and quart-size mayonnaise or salad dressing jars may be used with new two-piece lids for canning acid foods. However, you should expect more seal failures and jar breakage. These jars have a narrower sealing surface and are tempered less than Mason jars, and may be weakened by repeated contact with metal spoons or knives used in dispensing mayonnaise or salad dressing. Seemingly insignificant scratches in glass may cause cracking and breakage while processing jars in a canner. Mayonnaise-type jars are not recommended for use with foods to be processed in a pressure canner because of excessive jar breakage. Other commercial jars with mouths that cannot be sealed with two-piece canning lids are not recommended for use in canning any food at home.

Jar cleaning

Before every use, wash empty jars in hot water with detergent and rinse well by hand, or wash in a dishwasher. Unrinsed detergents may cause unnatural flavors and colors. These washing methods do not sterilize jars. Scale or hard-water films on jars are easily removed by soaking jars several hours in a solution containing 1 cup of vinegar (5 percent acidity) per gallon of water.

Sterilization of empty jars

All jams, jellies, and pickled products processed less than 10 minutes should be filled into sterile empty jars. To sterilize empty jars, put them right side up on the rack in a boiling-water canner. Fill the canner and jars with hot (not boiling) water to 1 inch above the tops of the jars. Boil 10 minutes at altitudes of less than 1,000 ft. At higher elevations, boil 1 additional minute for each additional 1,000 ft elevation. Remove and drain hot sterilized jars one at a time. Save the hot water for processing filled jars. Fill jars with food, add lids, and tighten screw bands.

Empty jars used for vegetables, meats, and fruits to be processed in a pressure canner need not be presterilized. It is also unnecessary to presterilize jars for fruits, tomatoes, and pickled or fermented foods that will be processed 10 minutes or longer in a boiling-water canner.

Lid selection, preparation, and use

The common self-sealing lid consists of a flat metal lid held in place by a metal screw band during processing. The flat lid is crimped around its bottom edge to form a trough, which is filled with a colored gasket compound. When jars are processed, the lid gasket softens and flows slightly to cover the jar-sealing surface, yet allows air to escape from the jar. The gasket then forms an airtight seal as the jar cools. Gaskets in unused lids work well for at least 5 years from date of manufacture. The gasket compound in older unused lids may fail to seal on jars.

Buy only the quantity of lids you will use in a year. To ensure a good seal, carefully follow the manufacturer's directions in preparing lids for use. Examine all metal lids carefully. Do not use old, dented, or deformed lids, or lids with gaps or other defects in the sealing gasket.

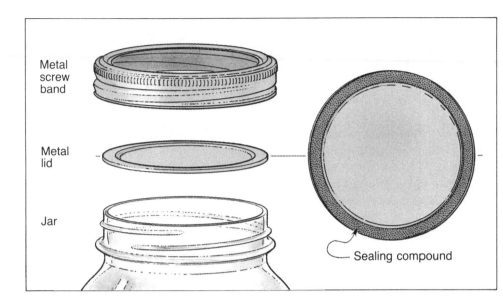

Metal screw band

Metal lid

Jar

Sealing compound

After filling jars with food, release air bubbles by inserting a flat plastic (not metal) spatula between the food and the jar. Slowly turn the jar and move the spatula up and down to allow air bubbles to escape. Adjust the headspace and then clean the jar rim (sealing surface) with a dampened paper towel. Place the lid, gasket down, onto the cleaned jar-sealing surface. Uncleaned jar-sealing surfaces may cause seal failures.

Then fit the metal screw band over the flat lid. Follow the manufacturer's guidelines enclosed with or on the box for tightening the jar lids properly.

Do not retighten lids after processing jars. As jars cool, the contents in the jar contract, pulling the self-sealing lid firmly against the jar to form a high vacuum.

- If rings are too loose, liquid may escape from jars during processing, and seals may fail.
- If rings are too tight, air cannot vent during processing, and food will discolor during storage. Overtightening also may cause lids to buckle and jars to break, especially with raw-packed, pressure-processed food.

Screw bands are not needed on stored jars. They can be removed easily after jars are cooled. When removed, washed, dried, and stored in a dry area, screw bands may be used many times. If left on stored jars, they become difficult to remove, often rust, and may not work properly again.

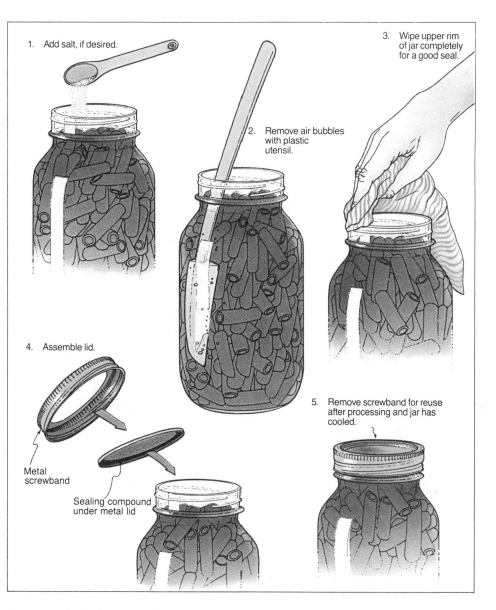

1. Add salt, if desired.

2. Remove air bubbles with plastic utensil.

3. Wipe upper rim of jar completely for a good seal.

4. Assemble lid.

Metal screwband

Sealing compound under metal lid

5. Remove screwband for reuse after processing and jar has cooled.

Recommended canners

Equipment for heat-processing home-canned food is of two main types—boiling-water canners and pressure canners. Most are designed to hold seven quart jars or eight to nine pints. Small pressure canners hold four quart jars; some large pressure canners hold 18 pint jars in two layers, but hold only seven quart jars. Pressure saucepans with smaller volume capacities are not recommended for use in canning. Small capacity pressure canners are treated in a similar manner as standard larger canners, and should be vented using the typical venting procedures.

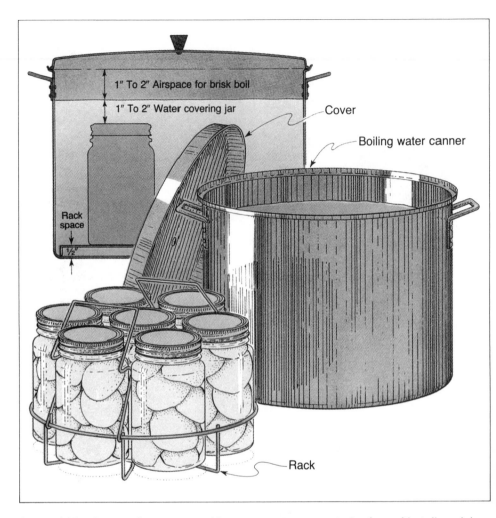

1" To 2" Airspace for brisk boil

1" To 2" Water covering jar

Cover

Boiling water canner

Rack space

½"

Rack

Low-acid foods must be processed in a pressure canner to be free of botulism risks. Although pressure canners may also be used for processing acid foods, boiling-water canners are recommended for this purpose because they are faster. A pressure canner would require from 55 to 100 minutes to process a load of jars; while the total time for processing most acid foods in boiling water varies from 25 to 60 minutes. A boiling-water canner loaded with filled jars requires about 20 to 30 minutes of heating before its water begins to boil. A loaded pressure canner requires about 12 to 15 minutes of heating before it begins to vent; another 10 minutes to vent the canner; another 5 minutes to pressurize the canner; another 8 to 10 minutes to process the acid food; and, finally, another 20 to 60 minutes to cool the canner before removing jars.

Boiling-water canners

These canners are made of aluminum or porcelain-covered steel. They have removable perforated racks and fitted lids. The canner must be deep enough so that at least 1 inch of briskly boiling water will be over the tops of jars during processing. Some boiling-water canners do not have flat bottoms. A flat bottom must be used on an electric range. Either a flat or ridged bottom can be used on a gas burner. To ensure uniform processing of all jars with an electric range, the canner should be no more than 4 inches wider in diameter than the element on which it is heated.

Using boiling-water canners

Follow these steps for successful boiling-water canning:
1. Fill the canner halfway with water.
2. Preheat water to 140°F for raw-packed foods and to 180°F for hot-packed foods.
3. Load filled jars, fitted with lids, into the canner rack and use the handles to lower the rack into the water; or fill the canner, one jar at a time, with a jar lifter.
4. Add more boiling water, if needed, so the water level is at least 1 inch above jar tops.
5. Turn heat to its highest position until water boils vigorously.
6. Set a timer for the minutes required for processing the food.
7. Cover with the canner lid and lower the heat setting to maintain a gentle boil throughout the process schedule.
8. Add more boiling water, if needed, to keep the water level above the jars.
9. When jars have been boiled for the recommended time, turn off the heat and remove the canner lid.
10. Using a jar lifter, remove the jars and place them on a towel, leaving at least 1-inch spaces between the jars during cooling.

Pressure canners

Pressure canners for use in the home have been extensively redesigned in recent years. Models made before the 1970's were heavy-walled kettles with clamp-on or turn-on lids. They were fitted with a dial gauge, a vent port in the form of a petcock or counterweight, and a safety fuse. Modern pressure canners are lightweight, thin-walled kettles; most have turn-on lids. They have a jar rack, gasket, dial or weighted gauge, an automatic vent/cover lock, a vent port (steam vent) to be closed with a counterweight or weighted gauge, and a safety fuse.

Pressure does not destroy microorganisms, but high temperatures applied for an adequate period of time do kill microorganisms. The success of destroying all microorganisms capable of growing in canned food is based on the temperature obtained in pure steam, free of air, at sea level. At sea level, a canner operated at a gauge pressure of 10.5 lbs provides an internal temperature of 240°F.

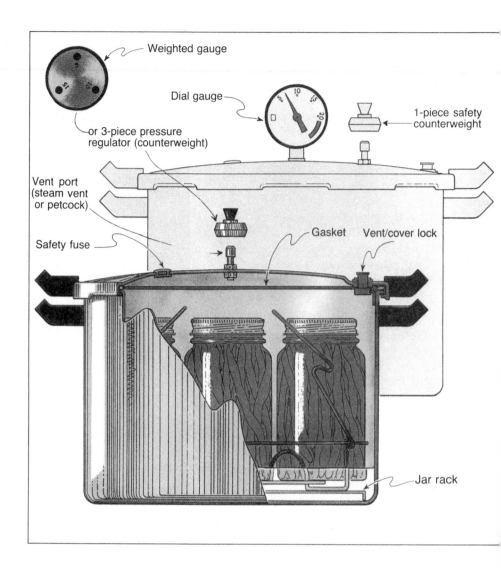

Two serious errors in temperatures obtained in pressure canners occur because:

1. **Internal canner temperatures are lower at higher altitudes.** To correct this error, canners must be operated at the increased pressures specified in this publication for appropriate altitude ranges.

2. **Air trapped in a canner lowers the temperature obtained at 5, 10, or 15 pounds of pressure and results in underprocessing.** The highest volume of air trapped in a canner occurs in processing raw-packed foods in dial-gauge canners. These canners do not vent air during processing. To be safe, all types of pressure canners must be vented 10 minutes before they are pressurized.

To vent a canner, leave the vent port uncovered on newer models or manually open petcocks on some older models. Heating the filled canner with its lid locked into place boils water and generates steam that escapes through the petcock or vent port. When steam first escapes, set a timer for 10 minutes. After venting 10 minutes, close the petcock or place the counterweight or weighted gauge over the vent port to pressurize the canner.

Weighted-gauge models exhaust tiny amounts of air and steam each time their gauge rocks or jiggles during processing. They control pressure precisely and need neither watching during processing nor checking for accuracy. The sound of the weight rocking or jiggling indicates that the canner is maintaining the recommended pressure. The single disadvantage of weighted-gauge canners is that they cannot correct precisely for higher altitudes. At altitudes above 1,000 feet, they must be operated at canner pressures of 10 instead of 5, or 15 instead of 10, PSI.

Check dial gauges for accuracy before use each year and replace if they read high by more than 1 pound at 5, 10, or 15 pounds of pressure. Low readings cause over-processing and may indicate that the accuracy of the gauge is unpredictable. Gauges may be checked at most county Cooperative Extension offices.

Handle canner lid gaskets carefully and clean them according to the manufacturer's directions. Nicked or dried gaskets will allow steam leaks during pressurization of canners. Keep gaskets clean between uses. Gaskets on older model canners may require a light coat of vegetable oil once per year. Gaskets on newer model canners are pre-lubricated and do not benefit from oiling. Check your canner's instructions if there is doubt that the particular gasket you use has been pre-lubricated.

Lid safety fuses are thin metal inserts or rubber plugs designed to relieve excessive pressure from the canner. Do not pick at or scratch fuses while cleaning lids. Use only canners that have the Underwriter's Laboratory (UL) approval to ensure their safety.

Replacement gauges and other parts for canners are often available at stores offering canning equipment or from canner manufacturers. When ordering parts, give your canner model number and describe the parts needed.

Using pressure canners

Follow these steps for successful pressure canning:

1. Put 2 to 3 inches of hot water in the canner. Place filled jars on the rack, using a jar lifter. Fasten canner lid securely.
2. Leave weight off vent port or open petcock. Heat at the highest setting until steam flows from the petcock or vent port.

Place 2"-3" of hot water in canner and place jars in canner on canner rack.

1.

Temperature

Exhaust all air from the cooker with vent port open.

2.

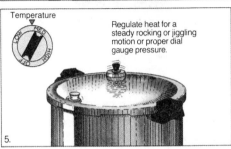

To pressurize the canner, place weight on vent port.

3.

Begin timing when weight starts to rock or jiggle, or when pressure gauge reads the correct pressure.

Time

4.

Temperature

Regulate heat for a steady rocking or jiggling motion or proper dial gauge pressure.

5.

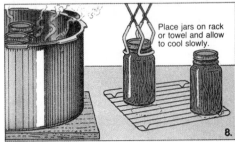

Remove from heat.

6.

After cooling, open vent port. Wait 2 minutes; then open cooker, lifting lid away from you.

7.

Place jars on rack or towel and allow to cool slowly.

8.

3. Maintain high heat setting, exhaust steam 10 minutes, and then place weight on vent port or close petcock. The canner will pressurize during the next 3 to 5 minutes.

4. Start timing the process when the pressure reading on the dial gauge indicates that the recommended pressure has been reached, or when the weighted gauge begins to jiggle or rock.

5. Regulate heat under the canner to maintain a steady pressure at or slightly above the correct gauge pressure. Quick and large pressure variations during processing may cause unnecessary liquid losses from jars. Weighted gauges on Mirro canners

should jiggle about 2 or 3 times per minute. On Presto canners, they should rock slowly throughout the process.

6. When the timed process is completed, turn off the heat, remove the canner from heat if possible, and let the canner depressurize. **Do not force-cool the canner.** Forced cooling may result in food spoilage. Cooling the canner with cold running water or opening the vent port before the canner is fully depressurized will cause loss of liquid from jars and seal failures. Force-cooling may also warp the canner lid of older model canners, causing steam leaks. Depressurization of older models should be timed. Standard-size heavy-walled canners require about 30 minutes when loaded with pints and 45 minutes with quarts. Newer thin-walled canners cool more rapidly and are equipped with vent locks. These canners are depressurized when their vent lock piston drops to a normal position.

7. After the canner is depressurized, remove the weight from the vent port or open the petcock. Wait 2 minutes, unfasten the lid, and remove it carefully. Lift the lid away from you so that the steam does not burn your face.

8. Remove jars with a lifter, and place on towel or cooling rack, if desired.

Selecting the correct processing time

When canning in boiling water, more processing time is needed for most raw-packed foods and for quart jars than is needed for hot-packed foods and pint jars.

To destroy microorganisms in acid foods processed in a boiling-water canner, you must:

• Process jars for the correct number of minutes in boiling water.
• Cool the jars at room temperature.

The food may spoil if you fail to add process time for lower boiling-water temperatures at altitudes above 1,000 feet, process for fewer minutes than specified, or cool jars in cold water.

To destroy microorganisms in low-acid foods processed with a pressure canner, you must:

• Process the jars using the correct time and pressure specified for your altitude.
• Allow canner to cool at room temperature until it is completely depressurized.

The food may spoil if you fail to select the proper process times for specific altitudes, fail to exhaust canners properly, process at lower pressure than specified, process for fewer minutes than specified, or cool the canner with water.

Using tables for determining proper process times

This set of guides includes processing times with altitude adjustments for each product. Process times for 1/2-pint and pint jars are the same. as are times for 1-1/2 pint and quart jars. For some products, you have a choice of processing at 5, 10, or 15 PSI. In these cases, choose the canner pressure you wish to use and match it with your pack style (raw or hot) and jar size to find the correct process time. The following examples show how to select the proper process for each type of canner. Process times are given in separate tables for sterilizing jars in boiling-water, dial-gauge and weighted-gauge pressure canners.

Example A: Boiling-water Canner

Suppose you are canning peaches as a hot-pack in quarts at 2,500 ft above sea level, using a *boiling-water canner.* First, select the process table for boiling-water canner. The example for peaches is given in **Table for Example A** on next page. From that table. select the process time given for (1) the style of pack (hot), (2) the jar size (quarts), and (3) the altitude where you live (2,500 ft). You should have selected a process time of 30 minutes.

Example B: Dial-gauge Pressure Canner

Suppose you are canning peaches as a hot-pack in quarts at 2,500 ft above sea level, using a *dial-gauge pressure canner.* First, select the process table for dial-gauge pressure canner. The example for peaches is given in **Table for Example B** on next page. From that table, select the process pressure (PSI) given for (1) style of pack (hot), (2) the jar size (quarts), (3) the process time (10 minutes), (4) the altitude where you live (2,500 ft). You should have selected a pressure of 7 lbs for the 10 minutes process time.

Example C: Weighted-gauge Pressure Canner

Suppose you are canning peaches as a hot-pack in quarts at 2,500 ft above sea level, using a *weighted-gauge pressure canner.* First, select the process table for weighted-gauge pressure canner. The example for peaches is given in **Table for Example C** on next page. From that table, select the process pressure (PSI) given for (1) style of pack (hot), (2) the jar size (quarts), (3) the process time (10 minutes), (4) the altitude where you live (2,500 ft). You should have selected a pressure of 10 lbs for the 10 minutes process time.

Table for Example A
Recommended process time for Peaches in a boiling-water canner

Style of Pack	Jar Size	Process Time at Altitudes of			
		0–1,000 ft	1,001–3,000 ft	3,001–6,000 ft	Above 6,000 ft
Hot	Pints	20 min	25 min	30 min	35 min
	Quarts	25	30	35	40
Raw	Pints	25	30	35	40
	Quarts	30	35	40	45

Table for Example B
Recommended process time for Peaches in a dial-gauge pressure canner

Style of Pack	Jar Size	Process Time	Canner Pressure (PSI) at Altitudes of			
			0–2,000 ft	2,001–4,000 ft	4,001–6,000 ft	6,001–8,000 ft
Hot and Raw	Pints or Quarts	10 mins	6 lb	7 lb	8 lb	9 lb

Table for Example C
Recommended process time for Peaches in a weighted-gauge pressure canner

Style of Pack	Jar Size	Process Time	Canner Pressure (PSI) at Altitudes of	
			0–1,000 ft	Above 1,000 ft
Hot and Raw	Pints or Quarts	10 mins	5 lb	10 lb

Cooling jars

When you remove hot jars from a canner, do not retighten their jar lids. Retightening of hot lids may cut through the gasket and cause seal failures. Cool the jars at room temperature for 12 to 24 hours. Jars may be cooled on racks or towels to minimize heat damage to counters. The food level and liquid volume of raw-packed jars will be noticeably lower after cooling. Air is exhausted during processing and food shrinks. If a jar loses excessive liquid during processing, do not open it to add more liquid. Check for sealed lids as described below.

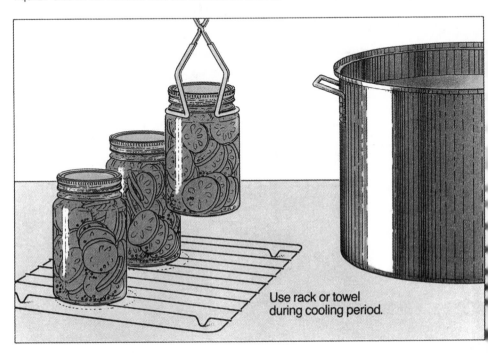

Use rack or towel during cooling period.

Testing jar seals

After cooling jars for 12 to 24 hours, remove the screw bands and test seals with one of the following options:

Option 1. Press the middle of the lid with a finger or thumb. If the lid springs up when you release your finger, the lid is unsealed.

Option 2. Tap the lid with the bottom of a teaspoon. If it makes a dull sound, the lid is not sealed. If food is in contact with the underside of the lid, it will also cause a dull sound. If the jar is sealed correctly, it will make a ringing, high-pitched sound.

Option 3. Hold the jar at eye level and look across the lid. The lid should be concave (curved down slightly in the center). If center of the lid is either flat or bulging, it may not be sealed.

Press the center of
lid with finger
or thumb

Listen for high-pitched
ring when lid is
tapped with
spoon

Note general
"concaveness" to lid

Reprocessing unsealed jars

If a lid fails to seal on a jar, remove the lid and check the jar-sealing surface for tiny nicks. If necessary, change the jar, add a new, properly prepared lid, and reprocess within 24 hours using the same processing time. Headspace in unsealed jars may be adjusted to 1-1/2 inches and jars could be frozen instead of reprocessed. Foods in single unsealed jars could be stored in the refrigerator and consumed within several days.

Storing canned foods

If lids are tightly vacuum sealed on cooled jars, remove screw bands, wash the lid and jar to remove food residue; then rinse and dry jars. Label and date the jars and store them in a clean, cool, dark, dry place. Do not store jars above 95°F or near hot pipes, a range, a furnace, in an uninsulated attic, or in direct sunlight. Under these conditions, food will lose quality in a few weeks or months and may spoil. Dampness may corrode metal lids, break seals, and allow recontamination and spoilage.

Accidental freezing of canned foods will not cause spoilage unless jars become unsealed and recontaminated. However, freezing and thawing may soften food. If jars must be stored where they may freeze, wrap them in newspapers, place them in heavy cartons, and cover with more newspapers and blankets.

Identifying and handling spoiled canned food

Do not taste food from a jar with an unsealed lid or food that shows signs of spoilage. You can more easily detect some types of spoilage in jars stored without screw bands. Growth of spoilage bacteria and yeast produces gas which pressurizes the food, swells lids, and breaks jar seals. As each stored jar is selected for use, examine its lid for tightness and vacuum. Lids with concave centers have good seals.

Next, while holding the jar upright at eye level, rotate the jar and examine its outside surface for streaks of dried food originating at the top of the jar. Look at the contents for rising air bubbles and unnatural color.

While opening the jar, smell for unnatural odors and look for spurting liquid and cottonlike mold growth (white, blue, black, or green) on the top food surface and underside of lid.

Spoiled low-acid foods, including tomatoes, may exhibit different kinds of spoilage evidence or very little evidence. Therefore, all suspect containers of spoiled low-acid foods, including tomatoes, should be treated as having produced botulinum toxin and handled carefully in one of two ways:
- If the swollen metal cans or suspect glass jars are still sealed, place them in a heavy garbage bag. Close and place the bag in a regular trash container or bury it in a nearby landfill.
- If the suspect cans or glass jars are unsealed, open, or leaking, they should be detoxified before disposal.

Detoxification process: Carefully place the suspect containers and lids on their sides in an 8-quart volume or larger stock pot, pan, or boiling-water canner. Wash your hands thoroughly. Carefully add water to the pot. The water should completely cover the containers with a minimum of a 1-inch level above the containers. Avoid splashing the water. Place a lid on the pot and heat the water to boiling. Boil 30 minutes to ensure detoxifying the food and all container components. Cool and discard the containers, their lids, and food in the trash or bury in soil.

Thoroughly scrub all counters, containers, and equipment including can opener, clothing, and hands that may have contacted the food or containers. Discard any sponges or wash cloths that may have been used in the cleanup. Place them in a plastic bag and discard in the trash.

Preparing pickled and fermented foods

The many varieties of pickled and fermented foods are classified by ingredients and method of preparation.

Regular dill pickles and sauerkraut are fermented and cured for about 3 weeks. Refrigerator dills are fermented for about 1 week. During curing, colors and flavors change and acidity increases. Fresh-pack or quick-process pickles are not fermented; some are brined several hours or overnight, then drained and covered with vinegar and seasonings. Fruit pickles usually are prepared by heating fruit in a seasoned syrup acidified with either lemon juice or vinegar. Relishes are made from chopped fruits and vegetables that are cooked with seasonings and vinegar.

Be sure to remove and discard a 1/16-inch slice from the blossom end of fresh cucumbers. Blossoms may contain an enzyme which causes excessive softening of pickles.

Caution: The level of acidity in a pickled product is as important to its safety as it is to taste and texture.

- **Do not alter vinegar, food, or water proportions in a recipe or use a vinegar with unknown acidity.**
- **Use only recipes with tested proportions of ingredients.**
- **There must be a minimum, uniform level of acid throughout the mixed product to prevent the growth of botulinum bacteria.**

Ingredients

Select fresh, firm fruits or vegetables free of spoilage. Measure or weigh amounts carefully, because the proportion of fresh food to other ingredients will affect flavor and, in many instances, safety.

Use canning or pickling salt. Noncaking material added to other salts may make the brine cloudy. Since flake salt varies in density, it is not recommended for making pickled and fermented foods. White granulated and brown sugars are most often used. Corn syrup and honey, unless called for in reliable recipes, may produce undesirable flavors. White distilled and cider vinegars of 5 percent acidity (50 grain) are recommended. White vinegar is usually preferred when light color is desirable, as is the case with fruits and cauliflower.

Pickles with reduced salt content

Recipes for pickles with reduced sodium content are provided in Guide 6.

In the making of fresh-pack pickles, cucumbers are acidified quickly with vinegar. Use only tested recipes formulated to produce the proper acidity. While these pickles may be prepared safely with reduced or no salt, their quality may be noticeably lower. Both texture and flavor may be slightly, but noticeably, different than expected. You may wish to make small quantities first to determine if you like them.

However, the salt used in making fermented sauerkraut and brined pickles not only provides characteristic flavor but also is vital to safety and texture. In fermented foods, salt favors the growth of desirable bacteria while inhibiting the growth of others. **Caution: Do not attempt to make sauerkraut or fermented pickles by cutting back on the salt required.**

Firming agents

Alum may be safely used to firm fermented pickles. However, it is unnecessary and is not included in the recipes in this publication. Alum does not improve the firmness of quick-process pickles. The calcium in lime definitely improves pickle firmness. Food-grade lime may be used as a lime-water solution for soaking fresh cucumbers 12 to 24 hours before pickling them. Excess lime absorbed by the cucumbers must be removed to make safe pickles. To remove excess lime, drain the lime-water solution, rinse, and then resoak the cucumbers in fresh water for 1 hour. Repeat the rinsing and soaking steps two more times. To further improve pickle firmness, you may process cucumber pickles for 30 minutes in water at 180°F. This process also prevents spoilage, **but the water temperature should not fall below 180°F.** Use a candy or jelly thermometer to check the water temperature.

Preventing spoilage

Pickle products are subject to spoilage from microorganisms, particularly yeasts and molds, as well as enzymes that may affect flavor, color, and texture. Processing the pickles in a boiling-water canner will prevent both of these problems. Standard canning jars and self-sealing lids are recommended. Processing times and procedures will vary according to food acidity and the size of food pieces.

Preparing butters, jams, jellies, and marmalades

Sweet spreads are a class of foods with many textures, flavors, and colors. They all consist of fruits preserved mostly by means of sugar and they are thickened or jellied to some extent. Fruit jelly is a semi-solid mixture of fruit juice and sugar that is clear and firm enough to hold its shape. Other spreads are made from crushed or ground fruit.

Jam also will hold its shape, but it is less firm than jelly. Jam is made from crushed or chopped fruits and sugar. Jams made from a mixture of fruits are usually called conserves, especially when they include citrus fruits, nuts, raisins, or coconut. Preserves are made of small, whole fruits or uniform-size pieces of fruits in a clear, thick, slightly jellied syrup. Marmalades are soft fruit jellies with small pieces of fruit or citrus peel evenly suspended in a transparent jelly. Fruit butters are made from fruit pulp cooked with sugar until thickened to a spreadable consistency.

Ingredients

For proper texture, jellied fruit products require the correct combination of fruit, pectin, acid, and sugar. The fruit gives each spread its unique flavor and color. It also supplies the water to dissolve the rest of the necessary ingredients and furnishes some or all of the pectin and acid. Good-quality, flavorful fruits make the best jellied products.

Pectins are substances in fruits that form a gel if they are in the right combination with acid and sugar. All fruits contain some pectin. Apples, crab apples, gooseberries, and some plums and grapes usually contain enough natural pectin to form a gel. Other fruits, such as strawberries, cherries, and blueberries, contain little pectin and must be combined with other fruits high in pectin or with commercial pectin products to obtain gels. Because fully ripened fruit has less pectin, one-fourth of the fruit used in making jellies without added pectin should be underripe.

Caution: Commercially frozen and canned juices may be low in natural pectins and make soft textured spreads.

The proper level of acidity is critical to gel formation. If there is too little acid, the gel will never set; if there is too much acid, the gel will lose liquid (weep). For fruits low in acid, add lemon juice or other acid ingredients as directed. Commercial pectin products contain acids which help to ensure gelling.

Sugar serves as a preserving agent, contributes flavor, and aids in gelling. Cane and beet sugar are the usual sources of sugar for jelly or jam. Corn syrup and honey may be used to replace part of the sugar in recipes, but too much will mask the fruit flavor and alter the gel structure. Use tested recipes for replacing sugar with honey and corn syrup. Do not try to reduce the amount of sugar in traditional recipes. Too little sugar prevents gelling and may allow yeasts and molds to grow.

Jams and jellies with reduced sugar

Jellies and jams that contain modified pectin, gelatin, or gums may be made with noncaloric sweeteners. Jams with less sugar than usual also may be made with concentrated fruit pulp, which contains less liquid and less sugar. See Guide 7 for recipes.

Two types of modified pectin are available for home use. One gels with one-third less sugar. The other is a low-methoxyl pectin which requires a source of calcium for gelling. To prevent spoilage, jars of these products must be processed longer in a boiling-water canner. Recipes and processing times provided with each modified pectin product must be followed carefully. The proportions of acids and fruits should not be altered, as spoilage may result.

Acceptably gelled refrigerator fruit spreads also may be made with gelatin and sugar substitutes. Such products spoil at room temperature, must be refrigerated, and should be eaten within 1 month.

Preventing spoilage

Even though sugar helps preserve jellies and jams, molds can grow on the surface of these products. Research now indicates that the mold which people usually scrape off the surface of jellies may not be as harmless as it seems. Mycotoxins have been found in some jars of jelly having surface mold growth. Mycotoxins are known to cause cancer in animals; their effects on humans are still being researched.

Because of possible mold contamination, paraffin or wax seals are no longer recommended for any sweet spread, including jellies. To prevent growth of molds and loss of good flavor or color, fill products hot into sterile Mason jars, leaving 1/4-inch headspace, seal with self-sealing lids, and process 5 minutes in a boiling-water canner. Correct process time at higher elevations by adding 1 additional minute per 1,000 ft above sea level. If unsterile jars are used, the filled jars should be processed 10 minutes. Use of sterile jars is preferred, especially when fruits are low in pectin, since the added 5-minute process time may cause weak gels. To sterilize empty jars, see page 15.

Methods of making jams and jellies

The two basic methods of making jams and jellies are described in Guide 7. The standard method, which does not require added pectin, works best with fruits naturally high in pectin. The other method, which requires the use of commercial liquid or powdered pectin, is much quicker. The gelling ability of various pectins differs. To make uniformly gelled products, be sure to add the quantities of commercial pectins to specific fruits as instructed on each package. Overcooking may break down pectin and prevent proper gelling. When using either method, make one batch at a time, according to the recipe. Increasing the quantities often results in soft gels. Stir constantly while cooking to prevent burning. Recipes are developed for specific jar sizes. If jellies are filled into larger jars, excessively soft products may result.

Canned foods for special diets

The cost of commercially canned special diet food often prompts interest in preparing these products at home. Some low-sugar and low-salt foods may be easily and safely canned at home. However, the color, flavor, and texture of these foods may be different than expected and be less acceptable.

Canning without sugar

In canning regular fruits without sugar, it is very important to select fully ripe but firm fruits of the best quality. Prepare these as described for hot-packs in Guide 2, but use water or regular unsweetened fruit juices instead of sugar syrup. Juice made from the fruit being canned is best. Blends of unsweetened apple, pineapple, and white grape juice are also good for filling over solid fruit pieces. Adjust head-spaces and lids and use the processing recommendations given for regular fruits. Add sugar substitutes, if desired, when serving.

Canning without salt (reduced sodium)

To can tomatoes, vegetables, meats, poultry, and seafood, use the procedures given in Guides 3 through 5, but omit the salt. In these products, salt seasons the food but is not necessary to ensure its safety. Add salt substitutes, if desired, when serving.

Canning fruit-based baby foods

You may prepare any chunk-style or pureed fruit with or without sugar, using the procedure for preparing each fruit as given in Guide 2. Pack in half-pint, preferably, or pint jars and use the following processing times.

Process time for fruit-based baby foods in a boiling-water canner

Style of Pack	Jar Size	Process Time at Altitudes of		
		0–1,000 ft	1,001–6,000 ft	Above 6,000 ft
Hot	Pints	20 min	25	30

Caution: Do not attempt to can pureed vegetables, red meats, or poultry meats, because proper processing times for pureed foods have not been determined for home use. Instead, can and store these foods using the standard processing procedures; puree or blend them at serving time. Heat the blended foods to boiling, simmer for 10 minutes, cool, and serve. Store unused portions in the refrigerator and use within 2 days for best quality.

How much should you can?

The amount of food to preserve for your family, either by canning or freezing, should be based on individual choices. The following table can serve as a worksheet to plan how much food you should can for use within a year.

Suggested Preservation Plan For Canned and Frozen Foods

Kind of Food	Serving Size	Servings/week[a]		My family needs				Quarts/year		
		Per person		My family[b]	Cups/week[c]	Qts/week[d]	Weeks served/yr[a]	Total[e]	Canned[a]	Frozen[a]
		Suggest	Actual							
Example: Family of 4										
Fruits	1/2 cup	12	12	48	24	6	36	216	72	144
My Plan:										
Fruits— apples, berries, peaches, plums, pears, tomatoes	1/2 cup	12								
Juices— apple, berry, grape, tomato	1 cup	7								
Vegetables— beets, beans, carrots, corn, peas, pumpkin, squash	1/2 cup	16								
Meat & Seafood— red meat, poultry, shellfish, fish	1/2 cup	14								
Soups	1 cup	2								
Pickles & Relishes— ketchup, fruit pickles, vegetable pickles, relish, etc.	—		1/2 cup							
Fruit Spreads— honey, jellies, jam, syrups, preserves, etc.	—		1/2 cup							
Sauces— tomato, etc.	1/2 cup	2								

a Your family should make these decisions.

b Servings/week for my family = actual weekly servings/person multiplied by number of family members who eat that food.

d Quarts/week = cups/week divided by 4.

e Total quarts/year = quarts/week multiplied by weeks served/year.

Glossary of Terms

Acid foods   Foods which contain enough acid to result in a pH of 4.6 or lower. Includes all fruits except figs; most tomatoes; fermented and pickled vegetables; relishes; and jams, jellies, and marmalades. Acid foods may be processed in boiling water.

Altitude   The vertical elevation of a location above sea level.

Ascorbic acid   The chemical name for vitamin C. Lemon juice contains large quantities of ascorbic acid and is commonly used to prevent browning of peeled, light-colored fruits and vegetables.

Bacteria   A large group of one-celled microorganisms widely distributed in nature. See microorganism.

Blancher   A 6- to 8-quart lidded pot designed with a fitted perforated basket to hold food in boiling water, or with a fitted rack to steam foods. Useful for loosening skins on fruits to be peeled, or for heating foods to be hot packed.

Boiling-water canner   A large standard-sized lidded kettle with jar rack, designed for heat-processing 7 quarts or 8 to 9 pints in boiling water.

Botulism   An illness caused by eating toxin produced by growth of *Clostridium botulinum* bacteria in moist, low-acid food, containing less than 2 percent oxygen, and stored between 40° and 120°F. Proper heat processing destroys this bacterium in canned food. Freezer temperatures inhibit its growth in frozen food. Low moisture controls its growth in dried food. High oxygen controls its growth in fresh foods.

Canning   A method of preserving food in air-tight vacuum-sealed containers and heat processing sufficiently to enable storing the food at normal home temperatures.

Canning salt   Also called pickling salt. It is regular table salt without the anticaking or iodine additives.

Citric acid   A form of acid that can be added to canned foods. It increases the acidity of low-acid foods and may improve the flavor and color.

Cold pack

Canning procedure in which jars are filled with raw food. "Raw pack" is the preferred term for describing this practice. "Cold pack" is often used incorrectly to refer to foods that are open-kettle canned or jars that are heat-processed in boiling water.

Enzymes

Proteins in food which accelerate many flavor, color, texture, and nutritional changes, especially when food is cut, sliced, crushed, bruised, and exposed to air. Proper blanching or hot-packing practices destroy enzymes and improve food quality.

Exhausting

Removal of air from within and around food and from jars and canners. Blanching exhausts air from live food tissues. Exhausting or venting of pressure canners is necessary to prevent a risk of botulism in low-acid canned foods.

Fermentation

Changes in food caused by intentional growth of bacteria, yeast, or mold. Native bacteria ferment natural sugars to lactic acid, a major flavoring and preservative in sauerkraut and in naturally fermented dills. Alcohol, vinegar, and some dairy products are also fermented foods.

Headspace

The unfilled space above food or liquid in jars. Allows for food expansion as jars are heated, and for forming vacuums as jars cool.

Heat processing

Treatment of jars with sufficient heat to enable storing food at normal home temperatures.

Hermetic seal

An absolutely airtight container seal which prevents reentry of air or microorganisms into packaged foods.

Hot pack

Heating of raw food in boiling water or steam and filling it hot into jars.

Low-acid foods

Foods which contain very little acid and have a pH above 4.6. The acidity in these foods is insufficient to prevent the growth of the bacterium *Clostridium botulinum*. Vegetables, some tomatoes, figs, all meats, fish, seafoods, and some dairy foods are low acid. To control all risks of botulism, jars of these foods must be (1) heat processed in a pressure canner, or (2) acidified to a pH of 4.6 or lower before processing in boiling water.

Microorganisms

Independent organisms of microscopic size, including bacteria, yeast, and mold. When alive in a suitable environment, they grow rapidly and may divide or reproduce every 10 to 30 minutes. Therefore, they reach high populations very quickly. Undesirable microorganisms cause disease and food spoilage. Microorganisms are sometimes intentionally added to ferment foods, make antibiotics, and for other reasons.

Mold

A fungus-type microorganism whose growth on food is usually visible and colorful. Molds may grow on many foods, including acid foods like jams and jellies and canned fruits. Recommended heat processing and sealing practices prevent their growth on these foods.

Mycotoxins

Toxins produced by the growth of some molds on foods.

Open-kettle canning

A non-recommended canning method. Food is supposedly adequately heat processed in a covered kettle, and then filled hot and sealed in sterile jars. Foods canned this way have low vacuums or too much air, which permits rapid loss of quality in foods. Moreover, these foods often spoil because they become recontaminated while the jars are being filled.

Pasteurization

Heating of a specific food enough to destroy the most heat-resistant pathogenic or disease-causing microorganism known to be associated with that food.

pH

A measure of acidity or alkalinity. Values range from 0 to 14. A food is neutral when its pH is 7.0: lower values are increasingly more acid; higher values are increasingly more alkaline.

Pickling

The practice of adding enough vinegar or lemon juice to a low-acid food to lower its pH to 4.6 or lower. Properly pickled foods may be safely heat processed in boiling water.

Pressure canner

A specifically designed metal kettle with a lockable lid used for heat processing low-acid food. These canners have jar racks, one or more safety devices, systems for exhausting air, and a way to measure or control pressure.

Canners with 20- to 21-quart capacity are common. The minimum volume of canner that can be used is 16-quart capacity, which will contain 7 quart jars. Use of pressure saucepans with less than 16-quart capacities is not recommended.

Raw pack

The practice of filling jars with raw, unheated food. Acceptable for canning low-acid foods, but allows more rapid quality losses in acid foods heat processed in boiling water.

Spice bag

A closeable fabric bag used to extract spice flavors in a pickling solution.

Style of pack

Form of canned food, such as whole, sliced, piece, juice, or sauce. The term may also be used to reveal whether food is filled raw or hot into jars.

Vacuum

The state of negative pressure. Reflects how thoroughly air is removed from within a jar of processed food—the higher the vacuum, the less air left in the jar.

Yeasts

A group of microorganisms which reproduce by budding. They are used in fermenting some foods and in leavening breads.

Index of Foods

Complete Guide to Home Canning, Guide 2

SELECTING, PREPARING, AND CANNING FRUIT AND FRUIT PRODUCTS

Guide 2

Selecting, Preparing, and Canning Fruit and Fruit Products

Table of Contents, Guide 2

Selecting, Preparing, and Canning Fruit and Fruit Products

General

Adding syrup to canned fruit helps to retain its flavor, color, and shape. It does not prevent spoilage of these foods. The following guidelines for preparing and using syrups offer a new "very light" syrup, which approximates the natural sugar content of many fruits. The sugar content in each of the five syrups is increased by about 10 percent. Quantities of water and sugar to make enough syrup for a canner load of pints or quarts are provided for each syrup type.

Preparing and using syrups

Syrup Type	Approx. % Sugar	Measures of Water and Sugar				Fruits commonly packed in syrup**
		For 9-Pt Load*		For 7-Qt Load		
		Cups Water	Cups Sugar	Cups Water	Cups Sugar	
Very Light	10	6-1/2	3/4	10-1/2	1-1/4	Approximates natural sugar level in most fruits and adds the fewest calories.
Light	20	5-3/4	1-1/2	9	2-1/4	Very sweet fruit. Try a small amount the first time to see if your family likes it.
Medium	30	5-1/4	2-1/4	8-1/4	3-3/4	Sweet apples, sweet cherries, berries, grapes.
Heavy	40	5	3-1/4	7-3/4	5-1/4	Tart apples, apricots, sour cherries, gooseberries, nectarines, peaches, pears, plums.
Very Heavy	50	4-1/4	4-1/4	6-1/2	6-3/4	Very sour fruit. Try a small amount the first time to see if your family likes it.

*This amount is also adequate for a 4-quart load.

**Many fruits that are typically packed in heavy syrup are excellent and tasteful products when packed in lighter syrups. It is recommended that lighter syrups be tried, since they contain fewer calories from added sugar.

Procedure: Heat water and sugar together. Bring to a boil and pour over raw fruits in jars. For hot packs, bring water and sugar to boil, add fruit, reheat to boil, and fill into jars immediately.

Other sweeteners: Light corn syrups or mild-flavored honey may be used to replace up to half the table sugar called for in syrups. See the section, "Canned foods for special diets," page 1·32, for further discussion.

APPLE BUTTER

Use Jonathan, Winesap, Stayman, Golden Delicious, MacIntosh, or other tasty apple varieties for good results.

8 lbs apples
2 cups cider
2 cups vinegar
2-1/4 cups white sugar
2-1/4 cups packed brown sugar
2 tbsp ground cinnamon
1 tbsp ground cloves

Yield: About 8 to 9 pints

Procedure: Wash, remove stems, quarter, and core fruit. Cook slowly in cider and
vinegar until soft. Press fruit through a colander, food mill, or strainer. Cook fruit
pulp with sugar and spices, stirring frequently. To test for doneness, remove a
spoonful and hold it away from steam for 2 minutes. It is done if the butter remains
mounded on the spoon. Another way to determine when the butter is cooked adequately is to spoon a small quantity onto a plate. When a rim of liquid does not separate around the edge of the butter, it is ready for canning. Fill hot into sterile half-
pint or pint jars, leaving 1/4-inch headspace. Quart jars need not be presterilized. To
presterilize jars, see page 1·15. Adjust lids and process.

Recommended process time for **Apple Butter** in a boiling-water
canner

Style of Pack	Jar Size	Process Time at Altitudes of		
		0– 1,000 ft	1,001– 6,000 ft	Above 6,000 ft
Hot	Half-pints or Pints	5 min	10	15
	Quarts	10	15	20

APPLE JUICE

Quality: Good quality apple juice is made from a blend of varieties. For best results,
buy fresh juice from a local cider maker within 24 hours after it has been pressed.

Procedure: Refrigerate juice for 24 to 48 hours. Without mixing, carefully pour off
clear liquid and discard sediment. Strain clear liquid through a paper coffee filter or
double layers of damp cheesecloth. Heat quickly, stirring occasionally, until juice
begins to boil. Fill immediately into sterile pint or quart jars (see page 1·15 to sterilize
jars), or fill into clean half-gallon jars, leaving 1/4-inch headspace. Adjust lids and
process.

Recommended process time for Apple Juice in a boiling-water canner

Style of Pack	Jar Size	Process Time at Altitudes of		
		0–1,000 ft	1,001–6,000 ft	Above 6,000 ft
Hot	Pints or Quarts	5 min	10	15
	Half-gallons	10	15	20

APPLE PIE FILLING See page 18

APPLES—SLICED

Quantity: An average of 19 pounds is needed per canner load of 7 quarts; an average of 12-1/4 pounds is needed per canner load of 9 pints. A bushel weighs 48 pounds and yields 16 to 19 quarts—an average of 2-3/4 pounds per quart.

Quality: Select apples that are juicy, crispy, and preferably both sweet and tart.

Procedure: Wash, peel, and core apples. To prevent discoloration, slice apples into water containing ascorbic acid (see page 1·11) Raw packs make poor quality products. Place drained slices in large saucepan and add 1 pint water or very light, light, or medium syrup (see page 5) per 5 pounds of sliced apples. Boil 5 minutes, stirring occasionally to prevent burning. Fill jars with hot slices and hot syrup or water, leaving 1/2-inch headspace. Adjust lids and process.

Recommended process time for Apples, sliced in a boiling-water canner

Style of Pack	Jar Size	Process Time at Altitudes of			
		0–1,000 ft	1,001–3,000 ft	3,001–6,000 ft	Above 6,000 ft
Hot	Pints or Quarts	20 min	25	30	35

Processing directions for canning sliced apples in a dial- or weighted-gauge canner are given on pages 26 and 27.

APPLESAUCE

Quantity: An average of 21 pounds is needed per canner load of 7 quarts; an average of 13-1/2 pounds is needed per canner load of 9 pints. A bushel weighs 48 pounds and yields 14 to 19 quarts of sauce—an average of 3 pounds per quart.

Quality: Select apples that are sweet, juicy, and crisp. For a tart flavor, add 1 to 2 pounds of tart apples to each 3 pounds of sweeter fruit.

Procedure: Wash, peel, and core apples. If desired, slice apples into water containing ascorbic acid (see page 1·11) to prevent browning. Placed drained slices in an 8- to 10-quart pot. Add 1/2 cup water. Stirring occasionally to prevent burning, heat quickly until tender (5 to 20 minutes, depending on maturity and variety). Press through a sieve or food mill, or skip the pressing step if you prefer chunk-style sauce. Sauce may be packed without sugar. If desired, add 1/8 cup sugar per quart of sauce. Taste and add more, if preferred. Reheat sauce to boiling. Fill jars with hot sauce, leaving 1/2-inch headspace. Adjust lids and process.

Recommended process time for Applesauce in a boiling-water canner

Style of Pack	Jar Size	Process Time at Altitudes of			
		0–1,000 ft	1,001–3,000 ft	3,001–6,000 ft	Above 6,000 ft
Hot	Pints	15 min	20	20	25
	Quarts	20	25	30	35

SPICED APPLE RINGS

12 lbs firm tart apples (maximum diameter, 2-1/2 inches)
12 cups sugar
6 cups water
1-1/4 cups white vinegar (5%)
3 tbsp whole cloves
3/4 cup red hot cinnamon candies or
  8 cinnamon sticks and
  1 tsp red food coloring (optional)

Yield: About 8 to 9 pints

Procedure: Wash apples. To prevent discoloration, peel and slice one apple at a time. Immediately cut crosswise into 1/2-inch slices, remove core area with a melon baller, and immerse in ascorbic acid solution (see page 1·11). To make flavored syrup combine sugar, water, vinegar, cloves, cinnamon candies, or cinnamon sticks and food coloring in a 6-qt saucepan. Stir, heat to boil, and simmer 3 minutes. Drain apples, add to hot syrup, and cook 5 minutes. Fill jars (preferably wide-mouth) with apple rings and hot flavored syrup, leaving 1/2-inch headspace. Adjust lids and process.

Recommended process time for Spiced Apple Rings in a boiling-water canner

Style of Pack	Jar Size	Process Time at Altitudes of		
		0–1,000 ft	1,001–6,000 ft	Above 6,000 ft
Hot	Half-pints or Pints	10 min	15	20

SPICED CRAB APPLES

5 lbs crab apples
4-1/2 cups apple vinegar (5%)
3-3/4 cups water
7-1/2 cups sugar
4 tsp whole cloves
4 sticks cinnamon
Six 1/2-inch cubes of fresh ginger root

Yield: About 9 pints

Procedure: Remove blossom petals and wash apples, but leave stems attached. Puncture the skin of each apple four times with an ice pick or toothpick. Mix vinegar, water, and sugar and bring to a boil. Add spices tied in a spice bag or cheesecloth. Using a blancher basket or sieve, immerse 1/3 of the apples at a time in the boiling vinegar/syrup solution for 2 minutes. Place cooked apples and spice bag in a clean 1- or 2-gallon crock and add hot syrup. Cover and let stand overnight. Remove spice bag, drain syrup into a large saucepan, and reheat to boiling. Fill pint jars with apples and hot syrup, leaving 1/2-inch headspace. Adjust lids and process.

Recommended process time for Spiced Crab Apples in a boiling-water canner

Style of Pack	Jar Size	Process Time at Altitudes of			
		0–1,000 ft	1,001–3,000 ft	3,001–6,000 ft	Above 6,000 ft
Hot	Pints	20 min	25	30	35

APRICOTS—HALVED OR SLICED

Quantity: An average of 16 pounds is needed per canner load of 7 quarts; an average of 10 pounds is needed per canner load of 9 pints. A bushel weighs 50 pounds and yields 20 to 25 quarts—an average of 2-1/4 pounds per quart.

Quality: Select firm, well-colored mature fruit of ideal quality for eating fresh.

Procedure: Follow directions for peaches. The boiling water dip and removal of skin process is optional. Wash fruit if skins are not removed; use either hot or raw pack, and the same process time. (See page 16.)

BERRIES—WHOLE

Blackberries, blueberries, currants, dewberries, elderberries, gooseberries, huckleberries, loganberries, mulberries, raspberries.

Quantity: An average of 12 pounds is needed per canner load of 7 quarts; an average of 8 pounds is needed per canner load of 9 pints. A 24-quart crate weighs 36 pounds and yields 18 to 24 quarts—an average of 1-3/4 pounds per quart.

Quality: Choose ripe, sweet berries with uniform color.

Procedure: Wash 1 or 2 quarts of berries at a time. Drain, cap, and stem if necessary. For gooseberries, snip off heads and tails with scissors. Prepare and boil preferred syrup (see page 5), if desired. Add 1/2 cup syrup, juice, or water to each clean jar.

Hot pack—For blueberries, currants, elderberries, gooseberries, and huckleberries. Heat berries in boiling water for 30 seconds and drain. Fill jars and cover with hot juice, leaving 1/2-inch headspace.

Raw pack—Fill jars with any of the raw berries, shaking down gently while filling. Cover with hot syrup, juice, or water, leaving 1/2-inch headspace.

Adjust lids and process.

Recommended process time for Berries, whole in a boiling-water canner

Style of Pack	Jar Size	Process Time at Altitudes of			
		0– 1,000 ft	1,001– 3,000 ft	3,001– 6,000 ft	Above 6,000 ft
Hot	Pints or Quarts	15 min	20	20	25
Raw	Pints	15	20	20	25
	Quarts	20	25	30	35

Processing directions for canning berries in a dial- or weighted-gauge canner are given on pages 26 and 27.

BERRY SYRUP

Juices from fresh or frozen blueberries, cherries, grapes, raspberries (black or red), and strawberries are easily made into toppings for use on ice cream and pastries.

Yield: About 9 half-pints.

Procedure: Select 6-1/2 cups of fresh or frozen fruit of your choice. Wash, cap, and stem fresh fruit and crush in a saucepan. Heat to boiling and simmer until soft (5 to 10 minutes). Strain hot through a colander and drain until cool enough to handle. Strain the collected juice through a double layer of cheesecloth or jelly bag. Discard the dry pulp. The yield of the pressed juice should be about 4-1/2 to 5 cups. Combine the juice with 6-3/4 cups of sugar in a large saucepan, bring to boil, and simmer 1 minute. To make a syrup with whole fruit pieces, save 1 or 2 cups of the fresh or frozen fruit, combine these with the sugar, and simmer as in making regular syrup. Remove from heat, skim off foam, and fill into clean half-pint or pint jars, leaving 1/2-inch headspace. Adjust lids and process.

Recommended process time for Berry Syrup in a boiling-water canner

Style of Pack	Jar Size	Process Time at Altitudes of		
		0–1,000 ft	1,001–6,000 ft	Above 6,000 ft
Hot	Half-pints or Pints	10 min	15	20

BLUEBERRY PIE FILLING (see page 19)

CHERRIES—WHOLE

Sweet or Sour

Quantity: An average of 17-1/2 pounds is needed per canner load of 7 quarts; an average of 11 pounds is needed per canner load of 9 pints. A lug weighs 25 pounds and yields 8 to 12 quarts—an average of 2-1/2 pounds per quart.

Quality: Select bright, uniformly colored cherries that are mature (of ideal quality for eating fresh or cooking).

Procedure: Stem and wash cherries. Remove pits if desired. If pitted, place cherries in water containing ascorbic acid (see page 1·11) to prevent stem-end discoloration. If canned unpitted, prick skins on opposite sides with a clean needle to prevent splitting. Cherries may be canned in water, apple juice, white grape juice, or syrup. If syrup is desired, select and prepare preferred type as directed on page 5.

Hot pack—In a large saucepan add 1/2 cup water, juice, or syrup for each quart of drained fruit and bring to boil. Fill jars with cherries and cooking liquid, leaving 1/2-inch headspace.

Raw pack—Add 1/2 cup hot water, juice, or syrup to each jar. Fill jars with drained cherries, shaking down gently as you fill. Add more hot liquid, leaving 1/2-inch headspace.

Adjust lids and process.

Recommended process time for Cherries, whole in a boiling-water canner

Style of Pack	Jar Size	Process Time at Altitudes of			
		0– 1,000 ft	1,001– 3,000 ft	3,001– 6,000 ft	Above 6,000 ft
Hot	Pints	15 min	20	20	25
	Quarts	20	25	30	35
Raw	Pints or Quarts	25	30	35	40

Processing directions for canning cherries in a dial- or weighted-gauge canner are given on pages 26 and 27.

FIGS

Quantity: An average of 16 pounds is needed per canner load of 7 quarts; an average of 11 pounds is needed per canner load of 9 pints—an average of 2-1/2 pounds yields 1 quart.

Quality: Select firm, ripe, uncracked figs. The mature color depends on the variety. Avoid overripe figs with very soft flesh.

Procedure: Wash figs thoroughly in clean water. Drain. Do not peel or remove stems. Cover figs with water and boil 2 minutes. Drain. Gently boil figs in light syrup (see page 5) for 5 minutes. **Add 2 tablespoons bottled lemon juice per quart or 1 tablespoon per pint to the jars; or add 1/2 teaspoon citric acid per quart or 1/4 teaspoon per pint to the jars.** Fill jars with hot figs and cooking syrup, leaving 1/2-inch headspace. Adjust lids and process.

Recommended process time for Figs in a boiling-water canner

Style of Pack	Jar Size	Process Time at Altitudes of			
		0– 1,000 ft	1,001– 3,000 ft	3,001– 6,000 ft	Above 6,000 ft
Hot	Pints	45 min	50	55	60
	Quarts	50	55	60	65

FRUIT PUREES of any fruit except figs and tomatoes

Procedure: Stem, wash, drain, peel, and remove pits if necessary. Measure fruit into large saucepan, crushing slightly if desired. Add 1 cup hot water for each quart of fruit. Cook slowly until fruit is soft, stirring frequently. Press through sieve or food mill. If desired for flavor, add sugar to taste. Reheat pulp to boil, or until sugar dissolves if added. Fill hot into clean jars, leaving 1/4-inch headspace. Adjust lids and process.

Recommended process time for Fruit Purees in a boiling-water canner

		Process Time at Altitudes of		
Style of Pack	Jar Size	0– 1,000 ft	1,001– 6,000 ft	Above 6,000 ft
Hot	Pints or Quarts	15 min	20	25

Processing directions for canning purees in a dial- or weighted-gauge canner are given on pages 26 and 27.

GRAPEFRUIT AND ORANGE SECTIONS

Quantity: An average of 15 pounds is needed per canner load of 7 quarts; an average of 13 pounds is needed per canner load of 9 pints—an average of about 2 pounds yields 1 quart.

Quality: Select firm, mature, sweet fruit of ideal quality for eating fresh. The flavor of orange sections is best if the sections are canned with equal parts of grapefruit. Grapefruit may be canned without oranges. Sections may be packed in your choice of water, citrus juice, or syrup.

Procedure: Wash and peel fruit and remove white tissue to prevent a bitter taste. If you use syrup, prepare a very light, light, or medium syrup (see page 5) and bring to boil. Fill jars with sections and water, juice, or hot syrup, leaving 1/2-inch headspace. Adjust lids and process.

Recommended process time for Grapefruit and Orange Sections in a boiling-water canner

		Process Time at Altitudes of		
Style of Pack	Jar Size	0– 1,000 ft	1,001– 6,000 ft	Above 6,000 ft
Raw	Pints or Quarts	10 min	15	20

Processing directions for canning citrus sections in a dial- or weighted-gauge canner are given on pages 26 and 27.

GRAPE JUICE

Quantity: An average of 24-1/2 pounds is needed per canner load of 7 quarts; an average of 16 pounds per canner load of 9 pints. A lug weighs 26 pounds and yields 7 to 9 quarts of juice—an average of 3-1/2 pounds per quart.

Quality: Select sweet, well-colored, firm, mature fruit of ideal quality for eating fresh or cooking.

Procedure: Wash and stem grapes. Place grapes in a saucepan and add boiling water to cover grapes. Heat and simmer slowly until skin is soft. Strain through a damp jelly bag or double layers of cheesecloth. Refrigerate juice for 24 to 48 hours. Without mixing, carefully pour off clear liquid and save; discard sediment. If desired, strain through a paper coffee filter for a clearer juice. Add juice to a saucepan and sweeten to taste. Heat and stir until sugar is dissolved. Continue heating with occasional stirring until juice begins to boil. Fill into jars immediately, leaving 1/4-inch headspace. (To sterilize empty pint and quart jars, see page 1·15) Adjust lids and process.

Recommended process time for Grape Juice in a boiling-water canner

Style of Pack	Jar Size	Process Time at Altitudes of		
		0–1,000 ft	1,001–6,000 ft	Above 6,000 ft
Hot	Pints or Quarts	5 min	10	15
	Half-gallons	10	15	20

GRAPES—WHOLE

Quantity: An average of 14 pounds is needed per canner load of 7 quarts; an average of 9 pounds is needed per canner load of 9 pints. A lug weighs 26 pounds and yields 12 to 14 quarts of whole grapes—an average of 2 pounds per quart.

Quality: Choose unripe, tight-skinned, preferably green seedless grapes harvested 2 weeks before they reach optimum eating quality.

Procedure: Stem, wash, and drain grapes. Prepare very light, or light syrup (see page 5).

Hot pack—Blanch grapes in boiling water for 30 seconds. Drain, and proceed as for raw pack.

Raw pack—Fill jars with grapes and hot syrup, leaving 1-inch headspace. Adjust lids and process.

Recommended process time for Grapes, whole in a boiling-water canner

Style of Pack	Jar Size	Process Time at Altitudes of			
		0–1,000 ft	1,001–3,000 ft	3,001–6,000 ft	Above 6,000 ft
Hot	Pints or Quarts	10 min	15	15	20
Raw	Pints	15	20	20	25
	Quarts	20	25	30	35

GREEN TOMATO PIE FILLING (see page 21)

MINCEMEAT PIE FILLING (see page 20)

MIXED FRUIT COCKTAIL

3 lbs peaches
3 lbs pears
1-1/2 lbs slightly underripe seedless green grapes
10-oz jar of maraschino cherries
3 cups sugar
4 cups water

Yield: About 6 pints

Procedure: Stem and wash grapes, and keep in ascorbic acid solution (see page 1·11). Dip ripe but firm peaches, a few at a time, in boiling water for 1 to 1-1/2 minutes to loosen skins. Dip in cold water and slip off skins. Cut in half, remove pits, cut into 1/2-inch cubes and keep in solution with grapes. Peel, halve, and core pears. Cut into 1/2-inch cubes, and keep in solution with grapes and peaches. Combine sugar and water in a saucepan and bring to boil. Drain mixed fruit. Add 1/2 cup of hot syrup to each jar. Then add a few cherries and gently fill the jar with mixed fruit and more hot syrup, leaving 1/2-inch headspace. Adjust lids and process.

Recommended process time for Mixed Fruit Cocktail in a boiling-water canner

Style of Pack	Jar Size	Process Time at Altitudes of			
		0–1,000 ft	1,001–3,000 ft	3,001–6,000 ft	Above 6,000 ft
Raw	Half-pints or Pints	20 min	25	30	35

NECTARINES—HALVED OR SLICED

Quantity: An average of 17-1/2 pounds is needed per canner load of 7 quarts; an average of 11 pounds is needed per canner load of 9 pints. A bushel weighs 48 pounds and yields 16 to 24 quarts—an average of 2-1/2 pounds per quart.

Quality: Choose ripe, mature fruit of ideal quality for eating fresh or cooking.

Procedure: Follow directions for peaches except do not dip in hot water or remove skins. Wash fruit and use either hot or raw pack and the same process time.

PEACHES—HALVED OR SLICED

Quantity: An average of 17-1/2 pounds is needed per canner load of 7 quarts; an average of 11 pounds is needed per canner load of 9 pints. A bushel weighs 48 pounds and yields 16 to 24 quarts—an average of 2-1/2 pounds per quart.

Quality: Choose ripe, mature fruit of ideal quality for eating fresh or cooking.

Procedure: Dip fruit in boiling water for 30 to 60 seconds until skins loosen. Dip quickly in cold water and slip off skins. Cut in half, remove pits and slice if desired. To prevent darkening, keep peeled fruit in ascorbic acid solution (see page 1·11). Prepare and boil a very light, light, or medium syrup (see page 5) or pack peaches in water, apple juice, or white grape juice. Raw packs make poor quality peaches.

Hot pack—In a large saucepan place drained fruit in syrup, water, or juice and bring to boil. Fill jars with hot fruit and cooking liquid, leaving 1/2-inch headspace. Place halves in layers, cut side down.

Raw pack—Fill jars with raw fruit, cut side down, and add hot water, juice, or syrup, leaving 1/2-inch headspace.

Adjust lids and process.

Recommended process time for Peaches, halved or sliced in a boiling-water canner

Style of Pack	Jar Size	Process Time at Altitudes of			
		0–1,000 ft	1,001–3,000 ft	3,001–6,000 ft	Above 6,000 ft
Hot	Pints	20 min	25	30	35
	Quarts	25	30	35	40
Raw	Pints	25	30	35	40
	Quarts	30	35	40	45

Processing directions for canning peaches in a dial- or weighted-gauge canner are given on pages 26 and 27.

PEACH PIE FILLING (see page 22)

PEARS—HALVED

Quantity: An average of 17-1/2 pounds is needed per canner load of 7 quarts; an average of 11 pounds is needed per canner load of 9 pints. A bushel weighs 50 pounds and yields 16 to 25 quarts—an average of 2-1/2 pounds per quart.

Quality: Choose ripe, mature fruit of ideal quality for eating fresh or cooking.

Procedure: Wash and peel pears. Cut lengthwise in halves and remove core. A melon baller or metal measuring spoon is suitable for coring pears. To prevent discoloration, keep pears in an ascorbic acid solution (see page 1·11). Prepare a very light, light, or medium syrup (see page 5) or pack pears in apple juice, white grape juice, or water. Raw packs make poor quality pears. Boil drained pears 5 minutes in syrup, juice, or water. Fill jars with hot fruit and cooking liquid, leaving 1/2-inch headspace. Adjust lids and process.

Recommended process time for Pears, halved in a boiling-water canner

Style of Pack	Jar Size	Process Time at Altitudes of			
		0–1,000 ft	1,001–3,000 ft	3,001–6,000 ft	Above 6,000 ft
Hot	Pints	20 min	25	30	35
	Quarts	25	30	35	40

Processing directions for canning pears in a dial- or weighted-gauge canner are given on pages 26 and 27.

PIE FILLINGS

General: The following fruit fillings are excellent and safe products. Each canned quart makes one 8-inch to 9-inch pie. The filling may be used as toppings on desserts or pastries. "Clear Jel®" is a chemically modified corn starch that produces excellent sauce consistency even after fillings are canned and baked. Other available starches break down when used in these pie fillings, causing a runny sauce consistency. Clear Jel® is available only through a few supply outlets and is not currently available in grocery stores. Find out about its availability prior to gathering other ingredients to make these pie fillings. If you cannot find it, ask your county Extension home economist about sources for Clear Jel®.

Because the variety of fruit may alter the flavor of the fruit pie, it is suggested that you first make a single quart, make a pie with it, and serve. Then adjust the sugar and spices in the recipe to suit your personal preferences. The amount of lemon juice should not be altered, as it aids in controlling the safety and storage stability of the fillings.

When using frozen cherries and blueberries, select unsweetened fruit. If sugar has been added, rinse it off while fruit is frozen. Thaw fruit, then collect, measure, and use juice from fruit to partially replace the water specified in the recipe. Use only 1/4 cup Clear Jel® per quart, or 1-3/4 cups for 7 quarts. Use fresh fruit in the apple and peach pie filling recipes.

APPLE PIE FILLING

| | Quantities of Ingredients Needed For | |
	1 Quart	7 Quarts
Blanched, sliced fresh apples	3-1/2 cups	6 quarts
Granulated sugar	3/4 cup + 2 tbsp	5-1/2 cups
Clear Jel®	1/4 cup	1-1/2 cups
Cinnamon	1/2 tsp	1 tbsp
Cold water	1/2 cup	2-1/2 cups
Apple juice	3/4 cup	5 cups
Bottled lemon juice	2 tbsp	3/4 cup
Nutmeg (optional)	1/8 tsp	1 tsp
Yellow food coloring (optional)	1 drop	7 drops

Quality: Use firm, crisp apples. Stayman, Golden Delicious, Rome, and other varieties of similar quality are suitable. If apples lack tartness, use an additional 1/4 cup of lemon juice for each 6 quarts of slices.

Yield: 1 quart or 7 quarts

Procedure: Wash, peel, and core apples. Prepare slices 1/2-inch wide and place in water containing ascorbic acid to prevent browning (see page 1-11). For fresh fruit, place 6 cups at a time in 1 gallon of boiling water. Boil each batch 1 minute after the water returns to a boil. Drain but keep heated fruit in a covered bowl or pot. Combine sugar, Clear Jel®, and cinnamon in a large kettle with water and apple juice. If desired, food coloring and nutmeg may be added. Stir and cook on medium high heat until mixture thickens and begins to bubble. Add lemon juice and boil 1 minute, stirring constantly. Fold in drained apple slices immediately and fill jars with mixture without delay, leaving 1-inch headspace. Adjust lids and process immediately.

Recommended process time for **Apple Pie Filling** in a
boiling-water canner

Style of Pack	Jar Size	Process Time at Altitudes of			
		0–1,000 ft	1,001–3,000 ft	3,001–6,000 ft	Above 6,000 ft
Hot	Pints or Quarts	25 min	30	35	40

BLUEBERRY PIE FILLING

	Quantities of Ingredients Needed For	
	1 Quart	**7 Quarts**
Fresh or thawed blueberries	*3-1/2 cups*	*6 quarts*
Granulated sugar	*3/4 cup + 2 tbsp*	*6 cups*
Clear Jel®	*1/4 cup + 1 tbsp*	*2-1/4 cups*
Cold water	*1 cup*	*7 cups*
Bottled lemon juice	*3-1/2 tsp*	*1/2 cup*
Blue food coloring (optional)	*3 drops*	*20 drops*
Red food coloring (optional)	*1 drop*	*7 drops*

Quality: Select fresh, ripe, and firm blueberries. Unsweetened frozen blueberries may be used. If sugar has been added, rinse it off while fruit is still frozen.

Yield: 1 quart or 7 quarts

Procedure: Wash and drain fresh blueberries. For fresh fruit, place 6 cups at a time in 1 gallon of boiling water. Boil each batch 1 minute after the water returns to a boil. Drain but keep heated fruit in a covered bowl or pot. Combine sugar and Clear Jel® in a large kettle. Stir. Add water and, if desired, food coloring. Cook on medium high heat until mixture thickens and begins to bubble. Add lemon juice and boil 1 minute, stirring constantly. Fold in drained berries immediately and fill jars with mixture without delay, leaving 1-inch headspace. Adjust lids and process immediately.

Recommended process time for **Blueberry Pie Filling** in a
boiling-water canner

Style of Pack	Jar Size	Process Time at Altitudes of			
		0–1,000 ft	1,001–3,000 ft	3,001–6,000 ft	Above 6,000 ft
Hot	Pints or Quarts	30 min	35	40	45

CHERRY PIE FILLING

	Quantities of Ingredients Needed For	
	1 Quart	7 Quarts
Fresh or thawed sour cherries	3-1/3 cups	6 quarts
Granulated sugar	1 cup	7 cups
Clear Jel®	1/4 cup + 1 tbsp	1-3/4 cups
Cold water	1-1/3 cups	9-1/3 cups
Bottled lemon juice	1 tbsp + 1 tsp	1/2 cup
Cinnamon (optional)	1/8 tsp	1 tsp
Almond extract (optional)	1/4 tsp	2 tsp
Red food coloring (optional)	6 drops	1/4 tsp

Quality: Select fresh, very ripe, and firm cherries. Unsweetened frozen cherries may be used. If sugar has been added, rinse it off while the fruit is still frozen.

Yield: 1 quart or 7 quarts

Procedure: Rinse and pit fresh cherries, and hold in cold water. To prevent stem end browning, use ascorbic acid solution (see page 1-11). For fresh fruit, place 6 cups at a time in 1 gallon boiling water. Boil each batch 1 minute after the water returns to a boil. Drain but keep heated in a covered bowl or pot. Combine sugar and Clear Jel® in a large saucepan and add water. If desired, add cinnamon, almond extract, and food coloring. Stir mixture and cook over medium high heat until mixture thickens and begins to bubble. Add lemon juice and boil 1 minute, stirring constantly. Fold in drained cherries immediately and fill jars with mixture without delay, leaving 1-inch headspace. Adjust lids and process immediately.

Recommended process time for Cherry Pie Filling in a boiling-water canner

		Process Time at Altitudes of			
Style of Pack	Jar Size	0– 1,000 ft	1,001– 3,000 ft	3,001– 6,000 ft	Above 6,000 ft
Hot	Pints or Quarts	30 min	35	40	45

FESTIVE MINCEMEAT PIE FILLING

2 cups finely chopped suet

4 lbs ground beef or 4 lb ground venison and 1 lb sausage

5 qts chopped apples

2 lbs dark seedless raisins

1 lb white raisins

2 qts apple cider

2 tbsp ground cinnamon

2 tsp ground nutmeg

5 cups sugar
2 tbsp salt

Yield: About 7 quarts

Procedure: Cook meat and suet in water to avoid browning. Peel, core, and quarter apples. Put meat, suet, and apples through food grinder using a medium blade. Combine all ingredients in a large saucepan, and simmer 1 hour or until slightly thickened. Stir often. Fill jars with mixture without delay, leaving 1-inch headspace. Adjust lids and process.

Recommended process time for Festive Mincemeat Pie Filling in a dial-gauge pressure canner

			Canner Pressure (PSI) at Altitudes of			
Style of Pack	Jar Size	Process Time	0– 2,000 ft	2,001– 4,000 ft	4,001– 6,000 ft	6,001– 8,000 ft
Hot	Quarts	90 min	11 lb	12 lb	13 lb	14 lb

Recommended process time for Festive Mincemeat Pie Filling in a weighted-gauge pressure canner

			Canner Pressure (PSI) at Altitudes of	
Style of Pack	Jar Size	Process Time	0– 1,000 ft	Above 1,000 ft
Hot	Quarts	90 min	10 lb	15 lb

GREEN TOMATO PIE FILLING

4 qts chopped green tomatoes
3 qts peeled and chopped tart apples
1 lb dark seedless raisins
1 lb white raisins
1/4 cup minced citron, lemon, or orange peel
2 cups water
2-1/2 cups brown sugar
2-1/2 cups white sugar
1/2 cup vinegar (5%)
1 cup bottled lemon juice
2 tbsp ground cinnamon
1 tsp ground nutmeg
1 tsp ground cloves

Yield: About 7 quarts

Procedure: Combine all ingredients in a large saucepan. Cook slowly, stirring often, until tender and slightly thickened (about 35 to 40 minutes). Fill jars with hot mixture, leaving 1/2-inch headspace. Adjust lids and process.

Recommended process time for Green Tomato Pie Filling in a boiling-water canner

Style of Pack	Jar Size	Process Time at Altitudes of		
		0–1,000 ft	1,001–6,000 ft	Above 6,000 ft
Hot	Quarts	15 min	20	25

PEACH PIE FILLING

	Quantities of Ingredients Needed For	
	1 Quart	7 Quarts
Sliced fresh peaches	3-1/2 cups	6 quarts
Granulated sugar	1 cup	7 cups
Clear Jel®	1/4 cup + 1 tbsp	2 cups + 3 tbsp
Cold water	3/4 cup	5-1/4 cups
Cinnamon (optional)	1/8 tsp	1 tsp
Almond extract (optional)	1/8 tsp	1 tsp
Bottled lemon juice	1/4 cup	1-3/4 cups

Quality: Select ripe, but firm fresh peaches. Red Haven, Redskin, Sun High, and other varieties of similar quality are suitable.

Yield: 1 quart or 7 quarts.

Procedure: Peel peaches. To loosen skins, submerge peaches in boiling water for approximately 30—60 seconds, and then place in cold water for 20 seconds. Slip off skins and prepare slices 1/2-inch thick. Place slices in water containing 1/2 tsp. of ascorbic acid crystals or six 500-milligram vitamin C tablets in 1 gallon of water to prevent browning. For fresh fruit, place 6 cups at a time in 1 gallon boiling water. Boil each batch 1 minute after the water returns to a boil. Drain but keep heated fruit in a covered bowl or pot. Combine water, sugar, Clear Jel® and, if desired, cinnamon and/or almond extract in a large kettle. Stir and cook over medium high heat until mixture thickens and begins to bubble. Add lemon juice and boil sauce 1 minute more, stirring constantly. Fold in drained peach slices and continue to heat mixture for 3 minutes. Fill jars without delay, leaving 1-inch headspace. Adjust lids and process immediately.

Recommended process time for Peach Pie Filling in a boiling-water canner

Style of Pack	Jar Size	Process Time at Altitudes of			
		0–1,000 ft	1,001–3,000 ft	3,001–6,000 ft	Above 6,000 ft
Hot	Pints or Quarts	30 min	35	40	45

PINEAPPLE

Quantity: An average of 21 pounds is needed per canner load of 7 quarts; an average of 13 pounds is needed per canner load of 9 pints—an average of 3 pounds per quart.

Quality: Select firm, ripe pineapples.

Procedure: Wash pineapple. Peel and remove eyes and tough fiber. Slice or cube. Pineapple may be packed in water, apple juice, white grape juice, or in very light, light, or medium syrup (see page 5). In a large saucepan, add pineapple to syrup, water, or juice, and simmer 10 minutes. Fill jars with hot pieces and cooking liquid, leaving 1/2-inch headspace. Adjust lids and process.

Recommended process time for Pineapple in a boiling-water canner

Style of Pack	Jar Size	Process Time at Altitudes of			
		0–1,000 ft	1,001–3,000 ft	3,001–6,000 ft	Above 6,000 ft
Hot	Pints	15 min	20	20	25
	Quarts	20	25	30	35

PLUMS—HALVED OR WHOLE

Quantity: An average of 14 pounds is needed per canner load of 7 quarts; an average of 9 pounds is needed per canner load of 9 pints. A bushel weighs 56 pounds and yields 22 to 36 quarts—an average of 2 pounds per quart.

Quality: Select deep-colored, mature fruit of ideal quality for eating fresh or cooking. Plums may be packed in water or syrup.

Procedure: Stem and wash plums. To can whole, prick skins on two sides of plums with fork to prevent splitting. Freestone varieties may be halved and pitted. If you use syrup, prepare very light, light, or medium syrup according to directions on page 5.

Hot pack—Add plums to water or hot syrup and boil 2 minutes. Cover saucepan and let stand 20 to 30 minutes. Fill jars with hot plums and cooking liquid or syrup, leaving 1/2-inch headspace.

Raw pack—Fill jars with raw plums, packing firmly. Add hot water or syrup, leaving 1/2-inch headspace.

Adjust lids and process.

Recommended process time for Plums, halved or whole in a boiling-water canner

Style of Pack	Jar Size	Process Time at Altitudes of			
		0–1,000 ft	1,001–3,000 ft	3,001–6,000 ft	Above 6,000 ft
Hot and Raw	Pints	20 min	25	30	35
	Quarts	25	30	35	40

Processing directions for canning plums in a dial- or weighted-gauge canner are given on pages 26 and 27.

RHUBARB—STEWED

Quantity: An average of 10-1/2 pounds is needed per canner load of 7 quarts; an average of 7 pounds is needed per canner load of 9 pints. A lug weighs 28 pounds and yields 14 to 28 quarts—an average of 1-1/2 pounds per quart.

Quality: Select young, tender, well-colored stalks from the spring or late fall crop.

Procedure: Trim off leaves. Wash stalks and cut into 1/2-inch to 1-inch pieces. In a large saucepan add 1/2 cup sugar for each quart of fruit. Let stand until juice appears. Heat gently to boiling. Fill jars without delay, leaving 1/2-inch headspace. Adjust lids and process.

Recommended process time for Rhubarb, stewed in a boiling-water canner

Style of Pack	Jar Size	Process Time at Altitudes of		
		0–1,000 ft	1,001–6,000 ft	Above 6,000 ft
Hot	Pints or Quarts	15 min	20	25

Process directions for canning rhubarb in a dial- or weighted-gauge canner are given on pages 26 and 27.

ZUCCHINI-PINEAPPLE

4 qts cubed or shredded zucchini
46 oz canned unsweetened pineapple juice
1-1/2 cups bottled lemon juice
3 cups sugar

Yield: About 8 to 9 pints

Procedure: Peel zucchini and either cut into 1/2-inch cubes or shred. Mix zucchini with other ingredients in a large saucepan and bring to a boil. Simmer 20 minutes. Fill jars with hot mixture and cooking liquid, leaving 1/2-inch headspace. Adjust lids and process.

Recommended process time for Zucchini-Pineapple in a boiling-water canner

Style of Pack	Jar Size	Process Time at Altitudes of		
		0–1,000 ft	1,001–6,000 ft	Above 6,000 ft
Hot	Half-pints or Pints	15 min	20	25

Process times for some acid foods in a dial-gauge pressure canner

Type of Fruit	Style of Pack	Jar Size	Process Time (Min)	Canner Pressure (PSI) at Altitudes of			
				0–2,000 ft	2,001–4,000 ft	4,001–6,000 ft	6,001–8,000 ft
Applesauce	Hot	Pints	8	6 lb	7 lb	8 lb	9 lb
	Hot	Quarts	10	6	7	8	9
Apples, sliced	Hot	Pints or Quarts	8	6	7	8	9
Berries, whole	Hot	Pints or Quarts	8	6	7	8	9
	Raw	Pints	8	6	7	8	9
	Raw	Quarts	10	6	7	8	9
Cherries, sour or sweet	Hot	Pints	8	6	7	8	9
	Hot	Quarts	10	6	7	8	9
	Raw	Pints or Quarts	10	6	7	8	9
Fruit Purees	Hot	Pints or Quarts	8	6	7	8	9
Grapefruit and Orange Sections	Hot	Pints or Quarts	8	6	7	8	9
	Raw	Pints	8	6	7	8	9
	Raw	Quarts	10	6	7	8	9
Peaches, Apricots, and Nectarines	Hot and Raw	Pints or Quarts	10	6	7	8	9
Pears	Hot	Pints or Quarts	10	6	7	8	9
Plums	Hot and Raw	Pints or Quarts	10	6	7	8	9
Rhubarb	Hot	Pints or Quarts	8	6	7	8	9

Process times for some acid foods in a weighted-gauge pressure canner

Type of Fruit	Style of Pack	Jar Size	Process Time (Min)	Canner Pressure (PSI) at Altitudes of	
				0–1,000 ft	Above 1,000 ft
Applesauce	Hot	Pints	8	5 lb	10 lb
	Hot	Quarts	10	5	10
Apples, sliced	Hot	Pints or Quarts	8	5	10
Berries, whole	Hot	Pints or Quarts	8	5	10
	Raw	Pints	8	5	10
	Raw	Quarts	10	5	10
Cherries, sour or sweet	Hot	Pints	8	5	10
	Hot	Quarts	10	5	10
	Raw	Pints or Quarts	10	5	10
Fruit Purees	Hot	Pints or Quarts	8	5	10
Grapefruit and Orange Sections	Hot	Pints or Quarts	8	5	10
	Raw	Pints	8	5	10
	Raw	Quarts	10	5	10
Peaches, Apricots, and Nectarines	Hot and Raw	Pints or Quarts	10	5	10
Pears	Hot	Pints or Quarts	10	5	10
Plums	Hot and Raw	Pints or Quarts	10	5	10
Rhubarb	Hot	Pints or Quarts	8	5	10

Complete Guide to Home Canning, Guide 3

SELECTING, PREPARING, AND CANNING TOMATOES AND TOMATO PRODUCTS

Guide 3

Selecting, Preparing, and Canning Tomatoes and Tomato Products

Table of Contents, Guide 3

Selecting, Preparing, and Canning Tomatoes and Tomato Products

General

Quality: Select only disease-free, preferably vine-ripened, firm fruit for canning. **Caution: Do not can tomatoes from dead or frost-killed vines. Green tomatoes are more acidic than ripened fruit and can be canned safely with any of the following recommendations.**

Acidification: To ensure safe acidity in whole, crushed, or juiced tomatoes, add two tablespoons of bottled lemon juice or 1/2 teaspoon of citric acid per quart of tomatoes. For pints, use one tablespoon bottled lemon juice or 1/4 teaspoon citric acid. Acid can be added directly to the jars before filling with product. Add sugar to offset acid taste, if desired. Four tablespoons of a 5 percent acidity vinegar per quart may be used instead of lemon juice or citric acid. However, vinegar may cause undesirable flavor changes.

Recommendation: Use of a pressure canner will result in higher quality and more nutritious canned tomato products. If your pressure canner cannot be operated above 15 PSI, select a process time at a lower pressure.

TOMATO JUICE

Quantity: An average of 23 pounds is needed per canner load of 7 quarts, or an average of 14 pounds per canner load of 9 pints. A bushel weighs 53 pounds and yields 15 to 18 quarts of juice—an average of 3-1/4 pounds per quart.

Procedure: Wash, remove stems, and trim off bruised or discolored portions. To prevent juice from separating, quickly cut about 1 pound of fruit into quarters and put directly into saucepan. Heat immediately to boiling while crushing. Continue to slowly add and crush freshly cut tomato quarters to the boiling mixture. Make sure the mixture boils constantly and vigorously while you add the remaining tomatoes. Simmer 5 minutes after you add all pieces.

If you are not concerned about juice separation, simply slice or quarter tomatoes into a large saucepan. Crush, heat, and simmer for 5 minutes before juicing.

Press both types of heated juice through a sieve or food mill to remove skins and seeds. **Add bottled lemon juice or citric acid to jars.** See acidification instructions on page 5. Heat juice again to boiling. Add 1 teaspoon of salt per quart to the jars, if desired. Fill jars with hot tomato juice, leaving 1/2-inch headspace. Adjust lids and process.

Recommended process time for Tomato Juice in a boiling-water canner

Style of Pack	Jar Size	Process Time at Altitudes of			
		0– 1,000 ft	1,001– 3,000 ft	3,001– 6,000 ft	Above 6,000 ft
Hot	Pints	35 min	40	45	50
	Quarts	40	45	50	55

Recommended process time for Tomato Juice in a dial-gauge pressure canner

Style of Pack	Jar Size	Process Time	Canner Gauge Pressure (PSI) at Altitudes of			
			0– 2,000 ft	2,001– 4,000 ft	4,001– 6,000 ft	6,001– 8,000 ft
Hot	Pints or	20 min	6 lb	7 lb	8 lb	9 lb
	Quarts	15	11	12	13	14

Recommended process time for Tomato Juice in a weighted-gauge pressure canner

Style of Pack	Jar Size	Process Time	Canner Gauge Pressure (PSI) at Altitudes of	
			0– 1,000 ft	Above 1,000 ft
Hot	Pints or	20 min	5 lb	10 lb
	Quarts	15	10	15
		10	15	Not Recommended

TOMATO AND VEGETABLE JUICE BLEND

Quantity: An average of 22 pounds of tomatoes is needed per canner load of 7 quarts. Not more than 3 cups of other vegetables may be added for each 22 pounds of tomatoes.

Procedure: Crush and simmer tomatoes as for making tomato juice (see page 5). Add no more than 3 cups of any combination finely chopped celery, onions, carrots, and peppers for each 22 pounds of tomatoes. Simmer mixture 20 minutes. Press hot cooked tomatoes and vegetables through a sieve or food mill to remove skins and seeds. **Add bottled lemon juice or citric acid to jars.** See acidification directions on page 5. Add 1 teaspoon of salt per quart to the jars, if desired. Reheat tomato-vegetable juice blend to boiling and fill immediately into jars, leaving 1/2-inch headspace. Adjust lids and process.

Recommended process time for Tomato-Vegetable Blend in a boiling-water canner

Style of Pack	Jar Size	Process Time at Altitudes of			
		0– 1,000 ft	1,001– 3,000 ft	3,001– 6,000 ft	Above 6,000 ft
Hot	Pints	35 min	40	45	50
	Quarts	40	45	50	55

Recommended process time for Tomato-Vegetable Blend in a dial-gauge pressure canner

Style of Pack	Jar Size	Process Time	Canner Gauge Pressure (PSI) at Altitudes of			
			0– 2,000 ft	2,001– 4,000 ft	4,001– 6,000 ft	6,001– 8,000 ft
Hot	Pints or	20 min	6 lb	7 lb	8 lb	9 lb
	Quarts	15	11	12	13	14

Recommended process time for Tomato-Vegetable Blend in a weighted-gauge pressure canner

Style of Pack	Jar Size	Process Time	Canner Gauge Pressure (PSI) at Altitudes of	
			0– 1,000 ft	Above 1,000 ft
Hot	Pints or	20 min	5 lb	10 lb
	Quarts	15	10	15
		10	15	Not Recommended

TOMATOES—CRUSHED (with no added liquid)

A high-quality product, ideally suited for use in soups, stews, and casseroles. This recipe is similar to that formerly referred to as "Quartered Tomatoes."

Quantity: An average of 22 pounds is needed per canner load of 7 quarts; an average of 14 fresh pounds is needed per canner load of 9 pints. A bushel weighs 53 pounds and yields 17 to 20 quarts of crushed tomatoes—an average of 2-3/4 pounds per quart.

Procedure: Wash tomatoes and dip in boiling water for 30 to 60 seconds or until skins split. Then dip in cold water, slip off skins, and remove cores. Trim off any bruised or discolored portions and quarter. Heat one-sixth of the quarters quickly in a large pot, crushing them with a wooden mallet or spoon as they are added to the pot. This will exude juice. Continue heating the tomatoes, stirring to prevent burning. Once the tomatoes are boiling, gradually add remaining quartered tomatoes, stirring constantly. These remaining tomatoes do not need to be crushed. They will soften with heating and stirring. Continue until all tomatoes are added. Then boil gently 5 minutes. **Add bottled lemon juice or citric acid to jars.** See acidification directions on page 5. Add 1 teaspoon of salt per quart to the jars, if desired. Fill jars immediately with hot tomatoes, leaving 1/2-inch headspace. Adjust lids and process.

Recommended process time for Crushed Tomatoes in a boiling-water canner

Style of Pack	Jar Size	Process Time at Altitudes of			
		0– 1,000 ft	1,001– 3,000 ft	3,001– 6,000 ft	Above 6,000 ft
Hot	Pints	35 min	40	45	50
	Quarts	45	50	55	60

Recommended process time for Crushed Tomatoes in a dial-gauge pressure canner

Style of Pack	Jar Size	Process Time	Canner Gauge Pressure (PSI) at Altitudes of			
			0– 2,000 ft	2,001– 4,000 ft	4,001– 6,000 ft	6,001– 8,000 ft
Hot	Pints or	20 min	6 lb	7 lb	8 lbs	9 lb
	Quarts	15	11	12	13	14

Recommended process time for Crushed Tomatoes in a weighted-gauge pressure canner

Style of Pack	Jar Size	Process Time	Canner Gauge Pressure (PSI) at Altitudes of	
			0– 1,000 ft	Above 1,000 ft
Hot	Pints or	20 min	5 lb	10 lb
	Quarts	15	10	15
		10	15	Not Recommended

STANDARD TOMATO SAUCE

Quantity: For thin sauce—An average of 35 pounds is needed per canner load of 7 quarts; an average of 21 pounds is needed per canner load of 9 pints. A bushel weighs 53 pounds and yields 10 to 12 quarts of sauce—an average of 5 pounds per quart. For thick sauce—An average of 46 pounds is needed per canner load of 7 quarts; an average of 28 pounds is needed per canner load of 9 pints. A bushel weighs 53 pounds and yields 7 to 9 quarts of sauce—an average of 6-1/2 pounds per quart.

Procedure: Prepare and press as for making tomato juice, see page 5. Simmer in large-diameter saucepan until sauce reaches desired consistency. Boil until volume is reduced by about one-third for thin sauce, or by one-half for thick sauce. **Add**

bottled lemon juice or citric acid to jars. See acidification directions on page 5. Add 1 teaspoon of salt per quart to the jars, if desired. Fill jars, leaving 1/4-inch headspace. Adjust lids and process.

Recommended process time for Standard Tomato Sauce in a boiling-water canner

Style of Pack	Jar Size	Process Time at Altitudes of			
		0–1,000 ft	1,001–3,000 ft	3,001–6,000 ft	Above 6,000 ft
Hot	Pints	35 min	40	45	50
	Quarts	40	45	50	55

Recommended process time for Standard Tomato Sauce in a dial-gauge pressure canner

Style of Pack	Jar Size	Process Time	Canner Gauge Pressure (PSI) at Altitudes of			
			0–2,000 ft	2,001–4,000 ft	4,001–6,000 ft	6,001–8,000 ft
Hot	Pints or Quarts	20 min	6 lb	7 lb	8 lb	9 lb
		15	11	12	13	14

Recommended process time for Standard Tomato Sauce in a weighted-gauge pressure canner

Style of Pack	Jar Size	Process Time	Canner Gauge Pressure (PSI) at Altitudes of	
			0–1,000 ft	Above 1,000 ft
Hot	Pints or Quarts	20 min	5 lb.	10 lb.
		15	10	15
		10	15	Not Recommended

TOMATOES—WHOLE OR HALVED (packed in water)

Quantity: An average of 21 pounds is needed per canner load of 7 quarts; an average of 13 pounds is needed per canner load of 9 pints. A bushel weighs 53 pounds and yields 15 to 21 quarts—an average of 3 pounds per quart.

Procedure for hot or raw tomatoes filled with water in jars: Wash tomatoes. Dip in boiling water for 30 to 60 seconds or until skins split; then dip in cold water. Slip off skins and remove cores. Leave whole or halve. **Add bottled lemon juice or citric acid to jars.** See acidification directions on page 5. Add 1 teaspoon of salt per quart to the jars, if desired. For hot pack products, add enough water to cover the tomatoes and boil them gently for 5 minutes. Fill jars with hot tomatoes or with raw peeled tomatoes. Add the hot cooking liquid to the hot pack, or hot water for raw pack to cover, leaving 1/2-inch headspace. Adjust lids and process.

Recommended process time for Water-Packed Whole Tomatoes in a boiling-water canner

Style of Pack	Jar Size	Process Time at Altitudes of			
		0–1,000 ft	1,001–3,000 ft	3,001–6,000 ft	Above 6,000 ft
Hot and Raw	Pints	40 min	45	50	55
	Quarts	45	50	55	60

Recommended process time for Water-Packed Whole Tomatoes in a dial-gauge pressure canner

Style of Pack	Jar Size	Process Time	Canner Gauge Pressure (PSI) at Altitudes of			
			0–2,000 ft	2,001–4,000 ft	4,001–6,000 ft	6,001–8,000 ft
Hot and Raw	Pints or Quarts	15 min	6 lb	7 lb	8 lb	9 lb
		10	11	12	13	14

Recommended process time for Water-Packed Whole Tomatoes in a weighted-gauge pressure canner

Style of Pack	Jar Size	Process Time	Canner Gauge Pressure (PSI) at Altitudes of	
			0–1,000 ft	Above 1,000 ft
Hot and Raw	Pints or Quarts	15 min	5 lb	10
		10	10	15
		1	15	Not Recommended

TOMATOES—WHOLE OR HALVED (packed in tomato juice)

Quantity: See whole tomatoes packed in water (page 9).

Procedure: Wash tomatoes. Dip in boiling water for 30 to 60 seconds or until skins split, then dip in cold water. Slip off skins and remove cores. Leave whole or halve. **Add bottled lemon juice or citric acid to the jars.** See acidification instructions on page 5. Add 1 teaspoon of salt per quart to the jars, if desired.

Raw pack—Heat tomato juice in a saucepan. Fill jars with raw tomatoes, leaving 1/2-inch headspace. Cover tomatoes in the jars with hot tomato juice, leaving 1/2-inch headspace.

Hot pack—Put tomatoes in a large saucepan and add enough tomato juice to completely cover them. Boil tomatoes and juice gently for 5 minutes. Fill jars with hot tomatoes, leaving 1/2-inch headspace. Add hot tomato juice to the jars to cover the tomatoes, leaving 1/2-inch headspace.

Adjust lids and process.

Recommended process time for Juice and Whole Tomatoes in a boiling-water canner

Style of Pack	Jar Size	Process Time at Altitudes of			
		0– 1,000 ft	1,001– 3,000 ft	3,001– 6,000 ft	Above 6,000 ft
Hot and Raw	Pints or Quarts	85 min	90	95	100

Recommended process time for Juice and Whole Tomatoes in a dial-gauge pressure canner

Style of Pack	Jar Size	Process Time	Canner Gauge Pressure (PSI) at Altitudes of			
			0– 2,000 ft	2,001– 4,000 ft	4,001– 6,000 ft	6,001– 8,000 ft
Hot and Raw	Pints or Quarts	40 min	6 lb	7 lb	8 lb	9 lb
		25	11	12	13	14

Recommended process time for Juice and Whole Tomatoes in a weighted-gauge pressure canner

Style of Pack	Jar Size	Process Time	Canner Gauge Pressure (PSI) at Altitudes of	
			0– 1,000 ft	Above 1,000 ft
Hot and Raw	Pints	40 min	5 lb	10 lb
		25	10	15
	Quarts	15	15	Not Recommended

TOMATOES—WHOLE OR HALVED (packed raw without added liquid)

Quantity: See whole tomatoes packed in water (page 9).

Procedure: Wash tomatoes. Dip in boiling water for 30 to 60 seconds or until skins split, then dip in cold water. Slip off skins and remove cores. Leave whole or halve. **Add bottled lemon juice or citric acid to the jars.** See acidification instructions on page 5. Add 1 teaspoon of salt per quart to the jars, if desired.

Fill jars with raw tomatoes, leaving 1/2-inch headspace. Press tomatoes in the jars until spaces between them fill with juice. Leave 1/2-inch headspace. Adjust lids and process.

Recommended process time for Raw Whole Tomatoes Without Added Liquid in a boiling-water canner

Style of Pack	Jar Size	Process Time at Altitudes of			
		0–1,000 ft	1,001–3,000 ft	3,001–6,000 ft	Above 6,000 ft
Raw	Pints or Quarts	85 min	90	95	100

Recommended process time for Raw Whole Tomatoes Without Added Liquid in a dial-gauge pressure canner

Style of Pack	Jar Size	Process Time	Canner Gauge Pressure (PSI) at Altitudes of			
			0–2,000 ft	2,001–4,000 ft	4,001–6,000 ft	6,001–8,000 ft
Raw	Pints or Quarts	40 min 25	6 lb 11	7 lb 12	8 lb 13	9 lb 14

Recommended process time for Raw Whole Tomatoes Without Added Liquid in a weighted-gauge pressure canner

Style of Pack	Jar Size	Process Time	Canner Gauge Pressure (PSI) at Altitudes of	
			0–1,000 ft	Above 1,000 ft
Raw	Pints or Quarts	40 min	5 lb	10 lb
		25	10	15
		15	15	Not Recommended

TOMATOES WITH OKRA OR ZUCCHINI

Quantity: An average of 12 pounds of tomatoes and 4 pounds of okra or zucchini is needed per canner load of 7 quarts. An average of 7 pounds of tomatoes and 2-1/2 pounds of okra or zucchini is needed per canner load of 9 pints.

Procedure: Wash tomatoes and okra or zucchini. Dip tomatoes in boiling water 30 to 60 seconds or until skins split. Then dip in cold water, slip off skins and remove cores, and quarter. Trim stems from okra and slice into 1-inch pieces or leave whole. Slice or cube zucchini if used. Bring tomatoes to a boil and simmer 10 minutes. Add okra or zucchini and boil gently 5 minutes. Add 1 teaspoon of salt for each quart to the jars, if desired. Fill jars with mixture, leaving 1-inch headspace. Adjust lids and process.

Variation: You may add four or five pearl onions or two onion slices to each jar.

Recommended process time for Tomatoes with Okra or Zucchini in a dial-gauge pressure canner

Style of Pack	Jar Size	Process Time	Canner Pressure (PSI) at Altitudes of			
			0–2,000 ft	2,001–4,000 ft	4,001–6,000 ft	6,001–8,000 ft
Hot	Pints	30 min	11 lb	12 lb	13 lb	14 lb
	Quarts	35	11	12	13	14

Recommended process time for Tomatoes with Okra or Zucchini in a weighted-gauge pressure canner

Style of Pack	Jar Size	Process Time	Canner Pressure (PSI) at Altitudes of	
			0–1,000 ft	Above 1,000 ft
Hot	Pints	30 min	10 lb	15 lb
	Quarts	35	10	15

SPAGHETTI SAUCE WITHOUT MEAT

30 lbs tomatoes
1 cup chopped onions
5 cloves garlic, minced
1 cup chopped celery or green pepper
1 lb fresh mushrooms, sliced (optional)
4-1/2 tsp salt
2 tbsp oregano
4 tbsp minced parsley
2 tsp black pepper
1/4 cup brown sugar
1/4 cup vegetable oil

Yield: About 9 pints

Procedure: Caution: Do not increase the proportion of onions, peppers, or mushrooms. Wash tomatoes and dip in boiling water for 30 to 60 seconds or until skins split. Dip in cold water and slip off skins. Remove cores and quarter tomatoes. Boil 20 minutes, uncovered, in large saucepan. Put through food mill or sieve. Saute onions, garlic, celery or peppers, and mushrooms (if desired) in vegetable oil until tender. Combine sauteed vegetables and tomatoes and add remainder of spices, salt, and sugar. Bring to a boil. Simmer, uncovered, until thick enough for serving. At this time the initial volume will have been reduced by nearly one-half. Stir frequently to avoid burning. Fill jars, leaving 1-inch headspace. Adjust lids and process.

Recommended process time for Spaghetti Sauce Without Meat in a dial-gauge pressure canner

Style of Pack	Jar Size	Process Time	Canner Gauge Pressure (PSI) at Altitudes of			
			0–2,000 ft	2,001–4,000 ft	4,001–6,000 ft	6,001–8,000 ft
Hot	Pints	20 min	11 lb	12 lb	13 lb	14 lb
	Quarts	25	11	12	13	14

Recommended process time for Spaghetti Sauce Without Meat in a weighted-gauge pressure canner

Style of Pack	Jar Size	Process Time	Canner Gauge Pressure (PSI) at Altitudes of	
			0–1,000 ft	Above 1,000 ft
Hot	Pints	20 min	10 lb	15 lb
	Quarts	25	10	15

SPAGHETTI SAUCE WITH MEAT

30 lbs tomatoes
2-1/2 lbs ground beef or sausage
5 cloves garlic, minced
1 cup chopped onions
1 cup chopped celery or green peppers
1 lb fresh mushrooms, sliced (optional)
4-1/2 tsp salt
2 tbsp oregano
4 tbsp minced parsley
2 tsp black pepper
1/4 cup brown sugar

Yield: About 9 pints

Procedure: To prepare tomatoes, follow directions for Spaghetti Sauce Without Meat, page 13. Saute beef or sausage until brown. Add garlic, onion, celery or green pepper, and mushrooms, if desired. Cook until vegetables are tender. Combine with tomato pulp in large saucepan. Add spices, salt, and sugar. Bring to a boil. Simmer, uncovered, until thick enough for serving. At this time initial volume will have been reduced by nearly one-half. Stir frequently to avoid burning. Fill jars, leaving 1-inch headspace. Adjust lids and process.

Recommended process time for Spaghetti Sauce With Meat in a dial-gauge pressure canner

Style of Pack	Jar Size	Process Time	Canner Gauge Pressure (PSI) at Altitudes of			
			0– 2,000 ft	2,001– 4,000 ft	4,001– 6,000 ft	6,001– 8,000 ft
Hot	Pints	60 min	11 lb	12 lb	13 lb	14 lb
	Quarts	70	11	12	13	14

Recommended process time for Spaghetti Sauce With Meat in a weighted-gauge pressure canner

Style of Pack	Jar Size	Process Time	Canner Gauge Pressure (PSI) at Altitudes of	
			0– 1,000 ft	Above 1,000 ft
Hot	Pints	60 min	10 lb	15 lb
	Quarts	70	10	15

MEXICAN TOMATO SAUCE

2-1/2 to 3 lbs chile peppers
18 lbs tomatoes
3 cups chopped onions
1 tbsp salt
1 tbsp oregano
1/2 cup vinegar

Yield: About 7 quarts

Procedure: Caution: Wear rubber gloves while handling chiles or wash hands thoroughly with soap and water before touching your face. Wash and dry chiles. Slit each pepper on its side to allow steam to escape. Peel peppers using one of the following methods:

Oven or broiler method: Place chiles in oven (400°F) or broiler for 6–8 minutes until skins blister.

Range-top method: Cover hot burner, either gas or electric, with heavy wire mesh. Place chiles on burner for several minutes until skins blister.

Allow peppers to cool. Place in a pan and cover with a damp cloth. This will make peeling the peppers easier. After several minutes, peel each pepper. Cool and slip off skins. Discard seeds and chop peppers. Wash tomatoes and dip in boiling water for 30 to 60 seconds or until skins split. Dip in cold water, slip off skins, and remove cores. Coarsely chop tomatoes and combine chopped peppers and remaining ingredients in large saucepan. Bring to a boil. Cover. Simmer 10 minutes. Fill jars, leaving 1-inch headspace. Adjust lids and process.

Recommended process time for Mexican Tomato Sauce in a dial-gauge pressure canner

Style of Pack	Jar Size	Process Time	Canner Gauge Pressure (PSI) at Altitudes of			
			0–2,000 ft	2,001–4,000 ft	4,001–6,000 ft	6,001–8,000 ft
Hot	Pints	20 min	11 lb	12 lb	13 lb	14 lb
	Quarts	25	11	12	13	14

Recommended process time for Mexican Tomato Sauce in a weighted-gauge pressure canner

Style of Pack	Jar Size	Process Time	Canner Pressure (PSI) at Altitudes of	
			0–1,000 ft	Above 1,000 ft
Hot	Pints	20 min	10 lb	15 lb
	Quarts	25	10	15

TOMATO KETCHUP

24 lbs ripe tomatoes
3 cups chopped onions
3/4 tsp ground red pepper (cayenne)
3 cups cider vinegar (5%)
4 tsp whole cloves
3 sticks cinnamon, crushed
1-1/2 tsp whole allspice
3 tbsp celery seeds
1-1/2 cups sugar
1/4 cup salt

Yield: 6 to 7 pints

Procedure: Wash tomatoes. Dip in boiling water for 30 to 60 seconds or until skins split. Dip in cold water. Slip off skins and remove cores. Quarter tomatoes into 4-gallon stock pot or a large kettle. Add onions and red pepper. Bring to boil and simmer 20 minutes, uncovered. Cover, turn off heat and let stand for 20 minutes. Combine spices in a spice bag and add to vinegar in a 2-quart saucepan. Bring to boil. Remove spice bag and combine vinegar and tomato mixture. Boil about 30 minutes. Put boiled mixture through a food mill or sieve. Return to pot. Add sugar and salt, boil gently, and stir frequently until volume is reduced by one-half or until mixture rounds up on spoon without separation. Fill pint jars, leaving 1/8-inch headspace. Adjust lids and process.

Recommended process time for Tomato Ketchup in a boiling-water canner

Style of Pack	Jar Size	Process Time at Altitudes of		
		0– 1,000 ft	1,001– 6,000 ft	Above 6,000 ft
Hot	Pints	15 min	20	25

COUNTRY WESTERN KETCHUP

24 lbs ripe tomatoes
5 chile peppers, sliced and seeded
1/4 cup salt
2-2/3 cups vinegar (5%)
1-1/4 cups sugar
1/2 tsp ground red pepper (cayenne)
4 tsp paprika
4 tsp whole allspice
4 tsp dry mustard
1 tbsp whole peppercorns
1 tsp mustard seeds
1 tbsp bay leaves

Yield: 6 to 7 pints

Procedure: Follow procedure and process time for regular tomato ketchup (page 16).

BLENDER KETCHUP

Use electric blender and eliminate need for pressing or sieving.

24 lbs ripe tomatoes
2 lbs onions
1 lb sweet red peppers
1 lb sweet green peppers
9 cups vinegar (5%)
9 cups sugar
1/4 cup canning or pickling salt
3 tbsp dry mustard
1-1/2 tbsp ground red pepper
1-1/2 tsp whole allspice
1-1/2 tbsp whole cloves
3 sticks cinnamon

Yield: About 9 pints

Procedure: Wash tomatoes and dip in boiling water for 30 to 60 seconds or until skins split. Then dip in cold water, slip off skins, core, and quarter. Remove seeds from peppers and slice into strips. Peel and quarter onions. Blend tomatoes, peppers, and onions at high speed for 5 seconds in electric blender. Pour into a 3- to 4-gallon stock pot or large kettle and heat. Boil gently 60 minutes, stirring frequently. Add vinegar, sugar, salt, and a spice bag containing dry mustard, red pepper, and other spices. Continue boiling and stirring until volume is reduced one-half and ketchup rounds up on a spoon with no separation of liquid and solids. Remove spice bag and fill jars, leaving 1/8-inch headspace. Adjust lids and follow process times for regular ketchup (see page 16).

CHILE SALSA (Hot Tomato-Pepper Sauce)

5 lbs tomatoes
2 lbs chile peppers
1 lb onions
1 cup vinegar (5%)
3 tsp salt
1/2 tsp pepper

Yield: 6 to 8 pints

Procedure: Caution: Wear rubber gloves while handling chiles or wash hands thoroughly with soap and water before touching your face. Peel and prepare chile peppers as described in making Mexican Tomato Sauce on page 15. Wash tomatoes and dip in boiling water for 30 to 60 seconds or until skins split. Dip in cold water, slip off skins, and remove cores. Coarsely chop tomatoes and combine chopped peppers, onions, and remaining ingredients in a large saucepan. Heat to boil, and simmer 10 minutes. Fill jars, leaving 1/2-inch headspace. Adjust lids and process.

Recommended process time for Chile Salsa in a boiling-water canner

Style of Pack	Jar Size	Process Time at Altitudes of		
		0–1,000 ft	1,001–6,000 ft	Above 6,000 ft
Hot	Pints	15 min	20	25

Complete Guide to Home Canning, Guide 4

SELECTING, PREPARING, AND CANNING VEGETABLES AND VEGETABLE PRODUCTS

Guide 4

Selecting, Preparing, and Canning Vegetables and Vegetable Products

Table of Contents, Guide 4

Selecting, Preparing, and Canning Vegetables and Vegetable Products

ASPARAGUS—SPEARS OR PIECES

Quantity: An average of 24-1/2 pounds is needed per canner load of 7 quarts; an average of 16 pounds is needed per canner load of 9 pints. A crate weighs 31 pounds and yields 7 to 12 quarts—an average of 3-1/2 pounds per quart.

Quality: Use tender, tight-tipped spears, 4 to 6 inches long.

Procedure: Wash asparagus and trim off tough scales. Break off tough stems and wash again. Cut into 1-inch pieces or can whole.

Hot pack—Cover asparagus with boiling water. Boil 2 or 3 minutes. Loosely fill jars with hot asparagus, leaving 1-inch headspace.

Raw pack—Fill jars with raw asparagus, packing as tightly as possible without crushing, leaving 1-inch headspace.

Add 1 teaspoon of salt per quart to the jars, if desired. Add boiling water, leaving 1-inch headspace. Adjust lids and process.

Recommended process time for Asparagus in a dial-gauge pressure canner

Style of Pack	Jar Size	Process Time	Canner Pressure (PSI) at Altitudes of			
			0–2,000 ft	2,001–4,000 ft	4,001–6,000 ft	6,001–8,000 ft
Hot and Raw	Pints	30 min	11 lb	12 lb	13 lb	14 lb
	Quarts	40	11	12	13	14

Recommended process time for Asparagus in a weighted-gauge pressure canner

Style of Pack	Jar Size	Process Time	Canner Pressure (PSI) at Altitudes of	
			0–1,000 ft	Above 1,000 ft
Hot and Raw	Pints	30 min	10 lb	15 lb
	Quarts	40	10	15

BEANS OR PEAS—SHELLED, DRIED

All varieties

Quantity: An average of 5 pounds is needed per canner load of 7 quarts; an average of 3-1/4 pounds is needed per canner load of 9 pints—an average of 3/4 pounds per quart.

Quality: Select mature, dry seeds. Sort out and discard discolored seeds.

Procedure: Place dried beans or peas in a large pot and cover with water. Soak 12 to 18 hours in a cool place. Drain water. To quickly hydrate beans, you may cover sorted and washed beans with boiling water in a saucepan. Boil 2 minutes, remove from heat, soak 1 hour and drain. Cover beans soaked by either method with fresh water and boil 30 minutes. Add 1/2 teaspoon of salt per pint or 1 teaspoon per quart to the jar, if desired. Fill jars with beans or peas and cooking water, leaving 1-inch headspace. Adjust lids and process.

Recommended process time for Beans or Peas in a dial-gauge pressure canner

Style of Pack	Jar Size	Process Time	Canner Pressure (PSI) at Altitudes of			
			0–2,000 ft	2,001–4,000 ft	4,001–6,000 ft	6,001–8,000 ft
Hot	Pints	75 min	11 lb	12 lb	13 lb	14 lb
	Quarts	90	11	12	13	14

Recommended process time for Beans or Peas in a weighted-gauge pressure canner

Style of Pack	Jar Size	Process Time	Canner Pressure (PSI) at Altitudes of	
			0–1,000 ft	Above 1,000 ft
Hot	Pints	75 min	10 lb	15 lb
	Quarts	90	10	15

BEANS, BAKED

Procedure: Soak and boil beans and prepare molasses sauce according to directions for beans with sauce on page 6. Place seven 3/4-inch pieces of pork, ham, or bacon in an earthenware crock, a large casserole, or a pan. Add beans and enough molasses sauce to cover beans. Cover and bake 4 to 5 hours at 350°F. Add water as needed—about every hour. Fill jars, leaving 1-inch headspace. Adjust lids and process as for beans with sauce on page 6.

BEANS, DRY, WITH TOMATO OR MOLASSES SAUCE

Quantity: An average of 5 pounds of beans is needed per canner load of 7 quarts; an average of 3-1/4 pounds is needed per canner load of 9 pints—an average of 3/4 pounds per quart.

Quality: Select mature, dry seeds. Sort out and discard discolored seeds.

Procedure: Sort and wash dry beans. Add 3 cups of water for each cup of dried beans or peas. Boil 2 minutes, remove from heat and soak 1 hour and drain. Heat to boiling in fresh water, and save liquid for making sauce. Make your choice of the following sauces:

Tomato Sauce—Either mix 1 quart tomato juice, 3 tablespoons sugar, 2 teaspoons salt, 1 tablespoon chopped onion, and 1/4 teaspoon each of ground cloves, allspice, mace, and cayenne pepper; or mix 1 cup tomato ketchup with 3 cups of cooking liquid from beans and heat to boiling.

Molasses Sauce—Mix 4 cups water or cooking liquid from beans, 3 tablespoons dark molasses, 1 tablespoon vinegar, 2 teaspoons salt, and 3/4 teaspoon powdered dry mustard. Heat to boiling.

Fill jars three-fourths full with hot beans. Add a 3/4-inch cube of pork, ham, or bacon to each jar, if desired. Fill jars with heated sauce, leaving 1-inch headspace. Adjust lids and process.

Recommended process time for Beans, Dry, with Tomato or Molasses Sauce in a dial-gauge pressure canner

Style of Pack	Jar Size	Process Time	Canner Pressure (PSI) at Altitudes of			
			0–2,000 ft	2,001–4,000 ft	4,001–6,000 ft	6,001–8,000 ft
Hot	Pints	65 min	11 lb	12 lb	13 lb	14 lb
	Quarts	75	11	12	13	14

Recommended process time for Beans, Dry, with Tomato or Molasses Sauce in a weighted-gauge pressure canner

Style of Pack	Jar Size	Process Time	Canner Pressure (PSI) at Altitudes of	
			0–1,000 ft	Above 1,000 ft
Hot	Pints	65 min	10 lb	15 lb
	Quarts	75	10	15

BEANS, FRESH LIMA—SHELLED

Quantity: An average of 28 pounds is needed per canner load of 7 quarts; an average of 18 pounds is needed per canner load of 9 pints. A bushel weighs 32 pounds and yields 6 to 10 quarts—an average of 4 pounds per quart.

Quality: Select well-filled pods with green seeds. Discard insect-damaged and diseased seeds.

Procedure: Shell beans and wash thoroughly.

Hot pack—Cover beans with boiling water and heat to boil. Fill jars loosely, leaving 1-inch headspace.

Raw pack—Fill jars with raw beans. Do not press or shake down.

Small beans—leave 1-inch of headspace for pints and 1-1/2 inches for quarts.

Large beans—leave 1-inch of headspace for pints and 1-1/4 inches for quarts.

Add 1 teaspoon of salt per quart to the jar, if desired. Add boiling water, leaving the same headspaces listed above. Adjust lids and process.

Recommended process time for Lima Beans in a dial-gauge pressure canner

Style of Pack	Jar Size	Process Time	Canner Pressure (PSI) at Altitudes of			
			0–2,000 ft	2,001–4,000 ft	4,001–6,000 ft	6,001–8,000 ft
Hot and Raw	Pints	40 min	11 lb	12 lb	13 lb	14 lb
	Quarts	50	11	12	13	14

Recommended process time for Lima Beans in a weighted-gauge pressure canner

Style of Pack	Jar Size	Process Time	Canner Pressure (PSI) at Altitudes of	
			0–1,000 ft	Above 1,000 ft
Hot and Raw	Pints	40 min	10 lb	15 lb
	Quarts	50	10	15

BEANS, SNAP AND ITALIAN—PIECES

Green and wax

Quantity: An average of 14 pounds is needed per canner load of 7 quarts; an average of 9 pounds is needed per canner load of 9 pints. A bushel weighs 30 pounds and yields 12 to 20 quarts—an average of 2 pounds per quart.

Quality: Select filled but tender, crisp pods. Remove and discard diseased and rusty pods.

Procedure: Wash beans and trim ends. Leave whole or cut or snap into 1-inch pieces.

Hot pack—Cover with boiling water; boil 5 minutes. Fill jars, loosely leaving 1-inch headspace.

Raw pack—Fill jars tightly with raw beans, leaving 1-inch headspace. Add 1 teaspoon of canning salt per quart to the jar, if desired. Add boiling water, leaving 1-inch headspace. Adjust lids and process.

Recommended process time for Snap and Italian Beans in a dial-gauge pressure canner

Style of Pack	Jar Size	Process Time	Canner Pressure (PSI) at Altitudes of			
			0–2,000 ft	2,001–4,000 ft	4,001–6,000 ft	6,001–8,000 ft
Hot and Raw	Pints	20 min	11 lb	12 lb	13 lb	14 lb
	Quarts	25	11	12	13	14

Recommended process time for Snap and Italian Beans in a weighted-gauge pressure canner

Style of Pack	Jar Size	Process Time	Canner Pressure (PSI) at Altitudes of	
			0–1,000 ft	Above 1,000 ft
Hot and Raw	Pints	20 min	10 lb	15 lb
	Quarts	25	10	15

BEETS—WHOLE, CUBED, OR SLICED

Quantity: An average of 21 pounds (without tops) is needed per canner load of 7 quarts; an average of 13-1/2 pounds is needed per canner load of 9 pints. A bushel (without tops) weighs 52 pounds and yields 15 to 20 quarts—an average of 3 pounds per quart.

Quality: Beets with a diameter of 1 to 2 inches are preferred for whole packs. Beets larger than 3 inches in diameter are often fibrous.

Procedure: Trim off beet tops, leaving an inch of stem and roots to reduce bleeding of color. Scrub well. Cover with boiling water. Boil until skins slip off easily; about 15 to 25 minutes depending on size. Cool, remove skins, and trim off stems and roots. Leave baby beets whole. Cut medium or large beets into 1/2-inch cubes or slices. Halve or quarter very large slices. Add 1 teaspoon of salt per quart to the jar, if desired. Fill jars with hot beets and fresh hot water, leaving 1-inch headspace. Adjust lids and process.

Recommended process time for Beets in a dial-gauge pressure canner

Style of Pack	Jar Size	Process Time	Canner Pressure (PSI) at Altitudes of			
			0–2,000 ft	2,001–4,000 ft	4,001–6,000 ft	6,001–8,000 ft
Hot	Pints	30 min	11 lb	12 lb	13 lb	14 lb
	Quarts	35	11	12	13	14

Recommended process time for Beets in a weighted-gauge pressure canner

Style of Pack	Jar Size	Process Time	Canner Pressure (PSI) at Altitudes of	
			0–1,000 ft	Above 1,000 ft
Hot	Pints	30 min	10 lb	15 lb
	Quarts	35	10	15

CARROTS—SLICED OR DICED

Quantity: An average of 17-1/2 pounds (without tops) is needed per canner load of 7 quarts; an average of 11 pounds is needed per canner load of 9 pints. A bushel (without tops) weighs 50 pounds and yields 17 to 25 quarts—an average of 2-1/2 pounds per quart.

Quality: Select small carrots, preferably 1 to 1-1/4 inches in diameter. Larger carrots are often too fibrous.

Procedure: Wash, peel, and rewash carrots. Slice or dice.

Hot pack—Cover with boiling water; bring to boil and simmer for 5 minutes. Fill jars, leaving 1-inch of headspace.

Raw pack—Fill jars tightly with raw carrots, leaving 1-inch headspace.

Add 1 teaspoon of salt per quart to the jar, if desired. Add hot cooking liquid or water, leaving 1-inch headspace. Adjust lids and process.

Recommended process time for Carrots in a dial-gauge pressure canner

Style of Pack	Jar Size	Process Time	Canner Pressure (PSI) at Altitudes of			
			0–2,000 ft	2,001–4,000 ft	4,001–6,000 ft	6,001–8,000 ft
Hot and Raw	Pints	25 min	11 lb	12 lb	13 lb	14 lb
	Quarts	30	11	12	13	14

Recommended process time for Carrots in a weighted-gauge pressure canner

Style of Pack	Jar Size	Process Time	Canner Pressure (PSI) at Altitudes of	
			0–1,000 ft	Above 1,000 ft
Hot and Raw	Pints	25 min	10 lb	15 lb
	Quarts	30	10	15

CORN—CREAM STYLE

Quantity: An average of 20 pounds (in husks) of sweet corn is needed per canner load of 9 pints. A bushel weighs 35 pounds and yields 12 to 20 pints—an average of 2-1/4 pounds per pint.

Quality: Select ears containing slightly immature kernels, or of ideal quality for eating fresh.

Procedure: Husk corn, remove silk, and wash ears. Blanch ears 4 minutes in boiling water. Cut corn from cob at about the center of kernel. Scrape remaining corn from cobs with a table knife.

Hot pack—To each quart of corn and scrapings, add two cups of boiling water. Heat to boiling. Add 1/2 teaspoon salt to each jar, if desired. Fill pint jar with hot corn mixture, leaving 1-inch headspace.

Recommended process time for Cream Style Corn in a dial-gauge pressure canner

Style of Pack	Jar Size	Process Time	Canner Pressure (PSI) at Altitudes of			
			0–2,000 ft	2,001–4,000 ft	4,001–6,000 ft	6,001–8,000 ft
Hot	Pints	85 min	11 lb	12 lb	13 lb	14 lb

Recommended process time for Cream Style Corn in a weighted-gauge pressure canner

Style of Pack	Jar Size	Process Time	Canner Pressure (PSI) at Altitudes of	
			0–1,000 ft	Above 1,000 ft
Hot	Pints	85 min	10 lb	15 lb

CORN—WHOLE KERNEL

Quantity: An average of 31-1/2 pounds (in husks) of sweet corn is needed per canner load of 7 quarts; an average of 20 pounds is needed per canner load of 9 pints. A bushel weighs 35 pounds and yields 6 to 11 quarts—an average of 4-1/2 pounds per quart.

Quality: Select ears containing slightly immature kernels or of ideal quality for eating fresh. Canning of some sweeter varieties or too immature kernels may cause browning. Can a small amount, check color and flavor before canning large quantities.

Procedure: Husk corn, remove silk, and wash. Blanch 3 minutes in boiling water. Cut corn from cob at about three-fourths the depth of kernel.

Caution: Do not scrape cob.

Hot pack—To each clean quart of kernels in a saucepan, add 1 cup of hot water, heat to boiling and simmer 5 minutes. Add 1 teaspoon of salt per quart to the jar, if desired. Fill jars with corn and cooking liquid, leaving 1-inch headspace.

Raw pack—Fill jars with raw kernels, leaving 1-inch headspace. Do not shake or press down. Add 1 teaspoon of salt per quart to the jar, if desired.

Add fresh boiling water, leaving 1-inch headspace. Adjust lids and process.

Recommended process time for Whole Kernel Corn in a dial-gauge pressure canner

Style of Pack	Jar Size	Process Time	Canner Pressure (PSI) at Altitudes of			
			0– 2,000 ft	2,001– 4,000 ft	4,001– 6,000 ft	6,001– 8,000 ft
Hot and Raw	Pints	55 min	11 lb	12 lb	13 lb	14 lb
	Quarts	85	11	12	13	14

Recommended process time for Whole Kernel Corn in a weighted-gauge pressure canner

Style of Pack	Jar Size	Process Time	Canner Pressure (PSI) at Altitudes of	
			0– 1,000 ft	Above 1,000 ft
Hot and Raw	Pints	55 min	10 lb	15 lb
	Quarts	85	10	15

MIXED VEGETABLES

6 cups sliced carrots
6 cups cut, whole kernel sweet corn
6 cups cut green beans
6 cups shelled lima beans
4 cups whole or crushed tomatoes
4 cups diced zucchini

Optional mix—You may change the suggested proportions or substitute other favorite vegetables except leafy greens, dried beans, cream-style corn, winter squash, or sweet potatoes.

Yield: 7 quarts

Procedure: Except for zucchini, wash and prepare vegetables as described for each vegetable on pages 10, 12, 8, 7; 3-9. Wash, trim, and slice or cube zucchini; combine all vegetables in a large pot or kettle, and add enough water to cover pieces. Add 1 teaspoon salt per quart to the jar, if desired. Boil 5 minutes and fill jars with hot pieces and liquid, leaving 1-inch headspace. Adjust lids and process.

Recommended process time for Mixed Vegetables in a dial-gauge pressure canner

Style of Pack	Jar Size	Process Time	Canner Pressure (PSI) at Altitudes of			
			0–2,000 ft	2,001–4,000 ft	4,001–6,000 ft	6,001–8,000 ft
Hot	Pints	75 min	11 lb	12 lb	13 lb	14 lb
	Quarts	90	11	12	13	14

Recommended process time for Mixed Vegetables in a weighted-gauge pressure canner

Style of Pack	Jar Size	Process Time	Canner Pressure (PSI) at Altitudes of	
			0–1,000 ft	Above 1,000 ft
Hot	Pints	75 min	10 lb	15 lb
	Quarts	90	10	15

MUSHROOMS—WHOLE OR SLICED

Quantity: An average of 14-1/2 pounds is needed per canner load of 9 pints; an average of 7-1/2 pounds is needed per canner load of 9 half-pints—an average of 2 pounds per pint.

Quality: Select only brightly colored, small to medium-size domestic mushrooms with short stems, tight veils (unopened caps), and no discoloration. **Caution: Do not can wild mushrooms.**

Procedure: Trim stems and discolored parts. Soak in cold water for 10 minutes to remove dirt. Wash in clean water. Leave small mushrooms whole; cut large ones. Cover with water in a saucepan and boil 5 minutes. Fill jars with hot mushrooms, leaving 1-inch headspace. Add 1/2 teaspoon of salt per pint to the jar, if desired. For better color, add 1/8 teaspoon of ascorbic acid powder, or a 500-milligram tablet of vitamin C. Add fresh hot water, leaving 1-inch headspace. Adjust lids and process.

Recommended process time for Mushrooms in a dial-gauge pressure canner

Style of Pack	Jar Size	Process Time	Canner Pressure (PSI) at Altitudes of			
			0– 2,000 ft	2,001– 4,000 ft	4,001– 6,000 ft	6,001– 8,000 ft
Hot	Half-pints or Pints	45 min	11 lb	12 lb	13 lb	14 lb

Recommended process time for Mushrooms in a weighted-gauge pressure canner

Style of Pack	Jar Size	Process Time	Canner Pressure (PSI) at Altitudes of	
			0– 1,000 ft	Above 1,000 ft
Hot	Half-pints or Pints	45 min	10 lb	15 lb

OKRA

Quantity: An average of 11 pounds is needed per canner load of 7 quarts; an average of 7 pounds is needed per canner load of 9 pints. A bushel weighs 26 pounds and yields 16 to 18 quarts—an average of 1-1/2 pounds per quart.

Quality: Select young, tender pods. Remove and discard diseased and rust-spotted pods.

Procedure: Wash pods and trim ends. Leave whole or cut into 1-inch pieces. Cover with hot water in a saucepan, boil 2 minutes and drain. Fill jars with hot okra and cooking liquid, leaving 1-inch headspace. Add 1 teaspoon of salt per quart to the jar, if desired. Adjust lids and process.

Recommended process time for Okra in a dial-gauge pressure canner

Style of Pack	Jar Size	Process Time	Canner Pressure (PSI) at Altitudes of			
			0–2,000 ft	2,001–4,000 ft	4,001–6,000 ft	6,001–8,000 ft
Hot	Pints	25 min	11 lb	12 lb	13 lb	14 lb
	Quarts	40	11	12	13	14

Recommended process time for Okra in a weighted-gauge pressure canner

Style of Pack	Jar Size	Process Time	Canner Pressure (PSI) at Altitudes of	
			0–1,000 ft	Above 1,000 ft
Hot	Pints	25 min	10 lb	15 lb
	Quarts	40	10	15

PEAS, GREEN OR ENGLISH—SHELLED

It is recommended that sugar snap and Chinese edible pods be frozen for best quality.

Quantity: An average of 31-1/2 pounds (in pods) is needed per canner load of 7 quarts; an average of 20 pounds is needed per canner load of 9 pints. A bushel weighs 30 pounds and yields 5 to 10 quarts—an average of 4-1/2 pounds per quart.

Quality: Select filled pods containing young, tender, sweet seeds. Discard diseased pods.

Procedure: Shell and wash peas. Add 1 teaspoon of salt per quart to the jar, if desired.

Hot pack—Cover with boiling water. Bring to a boil in a saucepan, and boil 2 minutes. Fill jars loosely with hot peas, and add cooking liquid, leaving 1-inch headspace.

Raw pack—Fill jars with raw peas, add boiling water, leaving 1-inch headspace. Do not shake or press down peas. Adjust lids and process.

Recommended process time for Peas in a dial-gauge pressure canner

Style of Pack	Jar Size	Process Time	Canner Pressure (PSI) at Altitudes of			
			0–2,000 ft	2,001–4,000 ft	4,001–6,000 ft	6,001–8,000 ft
Hot and Raw	Pints or Quarts	40 min	11 lb	12 lb	13 lb	14 lb

Recommended process time for Peas in a weighted-gauge pressure canner

Style of Pack	Jar Size	Process Time	Canner Pressure (PSI) at Altitudes of	
			0–1,000 ft	Above 1,000 ft
Hot and Raw	Pints or Quarts	40 min	10 lb	15 lb

PEPPERS

Hot or sweet, including chiles, jalapeno, and pimiento

Quantity: An average of 9 pounds is needed per canner load of 9 pints. A bushel weighs 25 pounds and yields 20 to 30 pints—an average of 1 pound per pint.

Quality: Select firm yellow, green, or red peppers. Do not use soft or diseased peppers.

Procedure: Select your favorite pepper(s). **Caution: If you choose hot peppers, wear plastic gloves while handling them or wash hands thoroughly with soap and water before touching your face.** Small peppers may be left whole. Large peppers may be quartered. Remove cores and seeds. Slash two or four slits in each pepper, and either blanch in boiling water or blister using one of the following methods:

Oven or broiler method: Place peppers in a hot oven (400°F) or broiler for 6–8 minutes until skins blister.

Range-top method: Cover hot burner, either gas or electric, with heavy wire mesh. Place peppers on burner for several minutes until skins blister.

Allow peppers to cool. Place in a pan and cover with a damp cloth. This will make peeling the peppers easier. After several minutes, peel each pepper. Flatten whole peppers. Add 1/2 teaspoon of salt to each pint jar, if desired. Fill jars loosely with peppers and add fresh boiled water, leaving 1-inch headspace. Adjust lids and process.

Recommended process time for Peppers in a dial-gauge pressure canner

Style of Pack	Jar Size	Process Time	Canner Pressure (PSI) at Altitudes of			
			0–2,000 ft	2,001–4,000 ft	4,001–6,000 ft	6,001–8,000 ft
Hot	Half-pints or Pints	35 min	11 lb	12 lb	13 lb	14 lb

Recommended process time for Peppers in a weighted-gauge pressure canner

| Style of Pack | Jar Size | Process Time | Canner Pressure (PSI) at Altitudes of | |
			0– 1,000 ft	Above 1,000 ft
Hot	Half-pints or Pints	35 min	10 lb	15 lb

POTATOES, SWEET—PIECES OR WHOLE

It is not recommended to dry pack sweet potatoes.

Quantity: An average of 17-1/2 pounds is needed per canner load of 7 quarts; an average of 11 pounds is needed per canner load of 9 pints. A bushel weighs 50 pounds and yields 17 to 25 quarts—an average of 2-1/2 pounds per quart.

Quality: Choose small to medium-sized potatoes. They should be mature and not too fibrous. Can within 1 to 2 months after harvest.

Procedure: Wash potatoes and boil or steam until partially soft (15 to 20 minutes). Remove skins. Cut medium potatoes, if needed, so that pieces are uniform in size. **Caution: Do not mash or puree pieces.** Fill jars, leaving 1-inch headspace. Add 1 teaspoon salt per quart to the jar, if desired. Cover with your choice of fresh boiling water or syrup (see page 2-5), leaving 1-inch headspace. Adjust lids and process.

Recommended process time for Sweet Potatoes in a dial-gauge pressure canner

| Style of Pack | Jar Size | Process Time | Canner Pressure (PSI) at Altitudes of | | | |
			0– 2,000 ft	2,001– 4,000 ft	4,001– 6,000 ft	6,001– 8,000 ft
Hot	Pints	65 min	11 lb	12 lb	13 lb	14 lb
	Quarts	90	11	12	13	14

Recommended process time for Sweet Potatoes in a weighted-gauge pressure canner

| Style of Pack | Jar Size | Process Time | Canner Pressure (PSI) at Altitudes of | |
			0– 1,000 ft	Above 1,000 ft
Hot	Pints	65 min	10 lb	15 lb
	Quarts	90	10	15

POTATOES, WHITE—CUBED OR WHOLE

Quantity: An average of 35 pounds is needed per canner load of 7 quarts; an average of 22-1/2 pounds is needed per canner load of 9 pints. A bag weighs 50 pounds and yields 8 to 12 quarts—an average of 5 pounds per quart.

Quality: Select small to medium-size mature potatoes of ideal quality for cooking. Tubers stored below 45°F may discolor when canned. Choose potatoes 1 to 2 inches in diameter if they are to be packed whole.

Procedure: Wash and peel potatoes. Place in ascorbic acid solution to prevent darkening (see page 1·11). If desired, cut into 1/2-inch cubes. Drain. Cook 2 minutes in boiling water and drain again. For whole potatoes, boil 10 minutes and drain. Add 1 teaspoon of salt per quart to the jar, if desired. Fill jars with hot potatoes and fresh hot water, leaving 1-inch headspace. Adjust lids and process.

Recommended process time for White Potatoes in a dial-gauge pressure canner

Style of Pack	Jar Size	Process Time	Canner Pressure (PSI) at Altitudes of			
			0–2,000 ft	2,001–4,000 ft	4,001–6,000 ft	6,001–8,000 ft
Hot	Pints	35 min	11 lb	12 lb	13 lb	14 lb
	Quarts	40	11	12	13	14

Recommended process time for White Potatoes in a weighted-gauge pressure canner

Style of Pack	Jar Size	Process Time	Canner Pressure (PSI) at Altitudes of	
			0–1,000 ft	Above 1,000 ft
Hot	Pints	35 min	10 lb	15 lb
	Quarts	40	10	15

PUMPKINS AND WINTER SQUASH—CUBED

Quantity: An average of 16 pounds is needed per canner load of 7 quarts; an average of 10 pounds is needed per canner load of 9 pints—an average of 2-1/4 pounds per quart.

Quality: Pumpkins and squash should have a hard rind and stringless, mature pulp of ideal quality for cooking fresh. Small size pumpkins (sugar or pie varieties) make better products.

Procedure: Wash, remove seeds, cut into 1-inch-wide slices, and peel. Cut flesh into 1-inch cubes. Boil 2 minutes in water. **Caution: Do not mash or puree.** Fill jars with cubes and cooking liquid, leaving 1-inch headspace. Adjust lids and process.

For making pies, drain jars and strain or sieve cubes.

Recommended process time for Pumpkin and Winter Squash in a dial-gauge pressure canner

Style of Pack	Jar Size	Process Time	Canner Pressure (PSI) at Altitudes of			
			0–2,000 ft	2,001–4,000 ft	4,001–6,000 ft	6,001–8,000 ft
Hot	Pints	55 min	11 lb	12 lb	13 lb	14 lb
	Quarts	90	11	12	13	14

Recommended process time for Pumpkin and Winter Squash in a weighted-gauge pressure canner

Style of Pack	Jar Size	Process Time	Canner Pressure (PSI) at Altitudes of	
			0–1,000 ft	Above 1,000 ft
Hot	Pints	55 min	10 lb	15 lb
	Quarts	90	10	15

SOUPS

Vegetable, dried bean or pea, meat, poultry, or seafoods

Procedure: Select, wash, and prepare vegetables, meat, and seafoods as described for the specific foods. Cover meat with water and cook until tender. Cool meat and remove bones. Cook vegetables. For each cup of dried beans or peas, add 3 cups of water, boil 2 minutes, remove from heat, soak 1 hour, and heat to boil. Drain and combine with meat broth, tomatoes, or water to cover. Boil 5 minutes. **Caution: Do not thicken.** Salt to taste, if desired. Fill jars halfway with solid mixture. Add remaining liquid, leaving 1-inch headspace. Adjust lids and process.

Recommended process time for Soups in a dial-gauge pressure canner

Style of Pack	Jar Size	Process Time	Canner Pressure (PSI) at Altitudes of			
			0–2,000 ft	2,001–4,000 ft	4,001–6,000 ft	6,001–8,000 ft
Hot	Pints	60* min	11 lb	12 lb	13 lb	14 lb
	Quarts	75*	11	12	13	14

*Caution: Process 100 minutes if soup contains seafoods.

**Recommended process time for Soups in a weighted-gauge
pressure canner**

| Style of Pack | Jar Size | Process Time | Canner Pressure (PSI) at Altitudes of | |
			0–1,000 ft	Above 1,000 ft
Hot	Pints	60* min	10 lb	15 lb
	Quarts	75*	10	15

*Caution: Process 100 minutes if soup contains seafoods.

SPINACH AND OTHER GREENS

Quantity: An average of 28 pounds is needed per canner load of 7 quarts; an average of 18 pounds is needed per canner load of 9 pints. A bushel weighs 18 pounds and yields 3 to 9 quarts—an average of 4 pounds per quart.

Quality: Can only freshly harvested greens. Discard any wilted, discolored, diseased, or insect-damaged leaves. Leaves should be tender and attractive in color.

Procedure: Wash only small amounts of greens at one time. Drain water and continue rinsing until water is clear and free of grit. Cut out tough stems and midribs. Place 1 pound of greens at a time in cheesecloth bag or blancher basket and steam 3 to 5 minutes or until well wilted. Add 1/2 teaspoon of salt to each quart jar, if desired. Fill jars loosely with greens and add fresh boiling water, leaving 1-inch headspace. Adjust lids and process.

**Recommended process time for Spinach and Other Greens in a
dial-gauge pressure canner**

| Style of Pack | Jar Size | Process Time | Canner Pressure (PSI) at Altitudes of | | | |
			0–2,000 ft	2,001–4,000 ft	4,001–6,000 ft	6,001–8,000 ft
Hot	Pints	70 min	11 lb	12 lb	13 lb	14 lb
	Quarts	90	11	12	13	14

**Recommended process time for Spinach and Other Greens in a
weighted-gauge pressure canner**

| Style of Pack | Jar Size | Process Time | Canner Pressure (PSI) at Altitudes of | |
			0–1,000 ft	Above 1,000 ft
Hot	Pints	70 min	10 lb	15 lb
	Quarts	90	10	15

SQUASH, WINTER—CUBED

Prepare and process according to instructions for "Pumpkin" (see page 18).

SUCCOTASH

15 lbs unhusked sweet corn or 3 qts cut whole kernels
14 lbs mature green podded lima beans or 4 qts shelled limas
2 qts crushed or whole tomatoes (optional)

Yield: 7 quarts

Procedure: Wash and prepare fresh produce as described for specific vegetables on pages 12 and 7; and 3·9.

Hot pack—Combine all prepared vegetables in a large kettle with enough water to cover the pieces. Add 1 teaspoon salt to each quart jar, if desired. Boil gently 5 minutes and fill jars with pieces and cooking liquid, leaving 1-inch headspace.

Raw pack—Fill jars with equal parts of all prepared vegetables, leaving 1-inch headspace. Do not shake or press down pieces. Add 1 teaspoon salt to each quart jar, if desired. Add fresh boiling water, leaving 1-inch headspace.

Adjust lids and process.

Recommended process time for Succotash in a dial-gauge pressure canner

Style of Pack	Jar Size	Process Time	Canner Pressure (PSI) at Altitudes of			
			0–2,000 ft	2,001–4,000 ft	4,001–6,000 ft	6,001–8,000 ft
Hot and Raw	Pints	60 min	11 lb	12 lb	13 lb	14 lb
	Quarts	85	11	12	13	14

Recommended process time for Succotash in a weighted-gauge pressure canner

Style of Pack	Jar Size	Process Time	Canner Pressure (PSI) at Altitudes of	
			0–1,000 ft	Above 1,000 ft
Hot and Raw	Pints	60 min	10 lb	15 lb
	Quarts	85	10	15

Complete Guide to Home Canning, Guide 5

PREPARING AND CANNING POULTRY, RED MEATS, AND SEAFOODS

Guide 5

Preparing and Canning Poultry, Red Meats, and Seafoods

Table of Contents, Guide 5

Preparing and Canning Poultry, Red Meats, and Seafoods

CHICKEN OR RABBIT

Procedure: Choose freshly killed and dressed, healthy animals. Large chickens are more flavorful than fryers. Dressed chicken should be chilled for 6 to 12 hours before canning. Dressed rabbits should be soaked 1 hour in water containing 1 tablespoon of salt per quart, and then rinsed. Remove excess fat. Cut the chicken or rabbit into suitable sizes for canning. Can with or without bones.

Hot pack—Boil, steam, or bake meat until about two-thirds done. Add 1 teaspoon salt per quart to the jar, if desired. Fill jars with pieces and hot broth, leaving 1-1/4-inch headspace.

Raw pack—Add 1 teaspoon salt per quart, if desired. Fill jars loosely with raw meat pieces, leaving 1-1/4-inch headspace. Do not add liquid.

Adjust lids and process.

Recommended process time for Chicken or Rabbit in a dial-gauge pressure canner

Style of Pack	Jar Size	Process Time	Canner Pressure (PSI) at Altitudes of			
			0–2,000 ft	2,001–4,000 ft	4,001–6,000 ft	6,001–8,000 ft
Without Bones:						
Hot and Raw	Pints	75 min	11 lb	12 lb	13 lb	14 lb
	Quarts	90	11	12	13	14
With Bones:						
Hot and Raw	Pints	65 min	11 lb	12 lb	13 lb	14 lb
	Quarts	75	11	12	13	14

Recommended process time for Chicken or Rabbit in a weighted-gauge pressure canner

Style of Pack	Jar Size	Process Time	Canner Pressure (PSI) at Altitudes of	
			0–1,000 ft	Above 1,000 ft
Without Bones:				
Hot and Raw	Pints	75 min	10 lb	15 lb
	Quarts	90	10	15
With Bones:				
Hot and Raw	Pints	65 min	10 lb	15 lb
	Quarts	75	10	15

GROUND OR CHOPPED MEAT

Bear, beef, lamb, pork, sausage, veal, venison

Procedure: Choose fresh, chilled meat. With venison, add one part high-quality pork fat to three or four parts venison before grinding. Use freshly made sausage, seasoned with salt and cayenne pepper (sage may cause a bitter off-flavor). Shape chopped meat into patties or balls or cut cased sausage into 3- to 4-inch links. Cook until lightly browned. Ground meat may be sauteed without shaping. Remove excess fat. Fill jars with pieces. Add boiling meat broth, tomato juice, or water, leaving 1-inch headspace. Add 1 teaspoon of salt per quart to the jars, if desired. Adjust lids and process.

Recommended process time for Ground or Chopped Meat in a dial-gauge pressure canner

Style of Pack	Jar Size	Process Time	Canner Pressure (PSI) at Altitudes of			
			0–2,000 ft	2,001–4,000 ft	4,001–6,000 ft	6,001–8,000 ft
Hot	Pints	75 min	11 lb	12 lb	13 lb	14 lb
	Quarts	90	11	12	13	14

Recommended process time for Ground or Chopped Meat in a weighted-gauge pressure canner

Style of Pack	Jar Size	Process Time	Canner Pressure (PSI) at Altitudes of	
			0–1,000 ft	Above 1,000 ft
Hot	Pints	75 min	10 lb	15 lb
	Quarts	90	10	15

STRIPS, CUBES, OR CHUNKS OF MEAT

Bear, beef, lamb, pork, veal, venison

Procedure: Choose quality chilled meat. Remove excess fat. Soak strong-flavored wild meats for 1 hour in brine water containing 1 tablespoon of salt per quart. Rinse. Remove large bones.

Hot pack—Precook meat until rare by roasting, stewing, or browning in a small amount of fat. Add 1 teaspoon of salt per quart to the jar, if desired. Fill jars with pieces and add boiling broth, meat drippings, water, or tomato juice (especially with wild game), leaving 1-inch headspace.

Raw pack—Add 1 teaspoon of salt per quart to the jar, if desired. Fill jars with raw meat pieces, leaving 1-inch headspace. Do not add liquid.

Adjust lids and process.

Recommended process time for Strips, Cubes, or Chunks of Meat in a dial-gauge pressure canner

Style of Pack	Jar Size	Process Time	Canner Pressure (PSI) at Altitudes of			
			0–2,000 ft	2,001–4,000 ft	4,001–6,000 ft	6,001–8,000 ft
Hot and Raw	Pints	75 min	11 lb	12 lb	13 lb	14 lb
	Quarts	90	11	12	13	14

Recommended process time for Strips, Cubes, or Chunks of Meat in a weighted-gauge pressure canner

Style of Pack	Jar Size	Process Time	Canner Pressure (PSI) at Altitudes of	
			0–1,000 ft	Above 1,000 ft
Hot and Raw	Pints	75 min	10 lb	15 lb
	Quarts	90	10	15

MEAT STOCK (BROTH)

Beef: Saw or crack fresh trimmed beef bones to enhance extraction of flavor. Rinse bones and place in a large stockpot or kettle, cover bones with water, add pot cover, and simmer 3 to 4 hours. Remove bones, cool broth, and pick off meat. Skim off fat, add meat removed from bones to broth, and reheat to boiling. Fill jars, leaving 1-inch headspace. Adjust lids and process.

Chicken or turkey: Place large carcass bones in a large stockpot, add enough water to cover bones, cover pot, and simmer 30 to 45 minutes or until meat can be easily stripped from bones. Remove bones and pieces, cool broth, strip meat, discard excess fat, and return meat to broth. Reheat to boiling and fill jars, leaving 1-inch headspace. Adjust lids and process.

Recommended process time for Meat Stock in a dial-gauge pressure canner

Style of Pack	Jar Size	Process Time	Canner Pressure (PSI) at Altitudes of			
			0–2,000 ft	2,001–4,000 ft	4,001–6,000 ft	6,001–8,000 ft
Hot	Pints	20 min	11 lb	12 lb	13 lb	14 lb
	Quarts	25	11	12	13	14

Recommended process time for Meat Stock in a weighted-gauge pressure canner

Style of Pack	Jar Size	Process Time	Canner Pressure (PSI) at Altitudes of	
			0–1,000 ft	Above 1,000 ft
Hot	Pints	20 min	10 lb	15 lb
	Quarts	25	10	15

CHILE CON CARNE

3 cups dried pinto or red kidney beans
5-1/2 cups water
5 tsp salt (separated)
3 lbs ground beef
1-1/2 cups chopped onions
1 cup chopped peppers of your choice (optional)
1 tsp black pepper
3 to 6 tbsp chili powder
2 qts crushed or whole tomatoes

Yield: 9 pints

Procedure: Wash beans thoroughly and place them in a 2 qt. saucepan. Add cold water to a level of 2 to 3 inches above the beans and soak 12 to 18 hours. Drain and discard water. Combine beans with 5-1/2 cups of fresh water and 2 teaspoons salt. Bring to a boil. Reduce heat and simmer 30 minutes. Drain and discard water. Brown ground beef, chopped onions, and peppers, if desired, in a skillet. Drain off fat and add 3 teaspoons salt, pepper, chili powder, tomatoes and drained cooked beans. Simmer 5 minutes. **Caution: Do not thicken.** Fill jars, leaving 1-inch headspace. Adjust lids and process.

Recommended process time for Chile Con Carne in a dial-gauge pressure canner

Style of Pack	Jar Size	Process Time	Canner Pressure (PSI) at Altitudes of			
			0–2,000 ft	2,001–4,000 ft	4,001–6,000 ft	6,001–8,000 ft
Hot	Pints	75 min	11 lb	12 lb	13 lb	14 lb

Recommended process time for Chile Con Carne in a weighted-gauge pressure canner

Style of Pack	Jar Size	Process Time	Canner Pressure (PSI) at Altitudes of	
			0–1,000 ft	Above 1,000 ft
Hot	Pints	75 min	10 lb	15 lb

CLAMS

Whole or minced

Procedure: Keep clams live on ice until ready to can. Scrub shells thoroughly and rinse, steam 5 minutes, and open. Remove clam meat. Collect and save clam juice. Wash clam meat in water containing 1 teaspoon of salt per quart. Rinse and cover clam meat with boiling water containing 2 tablespoons of lemon juice or 1/2 teaspoon of citric acid per gallon. Boil 2 minutes and drain. To make minced clams, grind clams with a meat grinder or food processor. Fill jars loosely with pieces and add hot clam juice and boiling water if needed, leaving 1-inch headspace. Adjust lids and process.

Recommended process time for Clams in a dial-gauge pressure canner

Style of Pack	Jar Size	Process Time	Canner Pressure (PSI) at Altitudes of			
			0– 2,000 ft	2,001– 4,000 ft	4,001– 6,000 ft	6,001– 8,000 ft
Hot	Half-pints	60 min	11 lb	12 lb	13 lb	14 lb
	Pints	70	11	12	13	14

Recommended process time for Clams in a weighted-gauge pressure canner

Style of Pack	Jar Size	Process Time	Canner Pressure (PSI) at Altitudes of	
			0– 1,000 ft	Above 1,000 ft
Hot	Half-pints	60 min	10 lb	15 lb
	Pints	70	10	15

KING AND DUNGENESS CRAB MEAT

It is recommended that blue crab meat be frozen for best quality.

Procedure: Keep live crabs on ice until ready to can. Wash crabs thoroughly, using several changes of cold water. Simmer crabs 20 minutes in water containing 1/4 cup of lemon juice and 2 tablespoons of salt (or up to 1 cup of salt, if desired) per gallon. Cool in cold water, drain, remove back shell, then remove meat from body and claws. Soak meat 2 minutes in cold water containing 2 cups of lemon juice or 4 cups of white vinegar, and 2 tablespoons of salt (or up to 1 cup of salt, if desired) per gallon. Drain and squeeze meat to remove excess moisture. Fill half-pint jars with 6 ounces of meat and pint jars with 12 ounces, leaving 1-inch headspace. Add 1/2 teaspoon of citric acid or 2 tablespoons of lemon juice to each half-pint jar, or 1 teaspoon of citric acid or 4 tablespoons of lemon juice per pint jar. Add hot water, leaving 1-inch headspace. Adjust lids and process.

Recommended process time for King and Dungeness Crab Meat in a dial-gauge pressure canner

Jar Size	Process Time	Canner Pressure (PSI) at Altitudes of			
		0– 2,000 ft	2,001– 4,000 ft	4,001– 6,000 ft	6,001– 8,000 ft
Half-pints	70 min	11 lb	12 lb	13 lb	14 lb
Pints	80	11	12	13	14

Recommended process time for King and Dungeness Crab Meat in a weighted-gauge pressure canner

Jar Size	Process Time	Canner Pressure (PSI) at Altitudes of	
		0– 1,000 ft	Above 1,000 ft
Half-pints	70 min	10 lb	15 lb
Pints	80	10	15

FISH

Blue, mackerel, salmon, steelhead, trout, and other fatty fish except tuna

Caution: Eviscerate fish within 2 hours after they are caught. Keep cleaned fish on ice until ready to can.

Note: Glass-like crystals of magnesium ammonium phosphate sometimes form in canned salmon. There is no way for the home canner to prevent these crystals from forming, but they usually dissolve when heated and are safe to eat.

Procedure: Remove head, tail, fins, and scales. Wash and remove all blood. Split fish lengthwise, if desired. Cut cleaned fish into 3-1/2-inch lengths. Fill pint jars, skin side next to glass, leaving 1-inch headspace. Add 1 teaspoon of salt per pint, if desired. Do not add liquids. Adjust lids and process.

Recommended process time for Fish in a dial-gauge pressure canner

Style of Pack	Jar Size	Process Time	Canner Pressure (PSI) at Altitudes of			
			0– 2,000 ft	2,001– 4,000 ft	4,001– 6,000 ft	6,001– 8,000 ft
Raw	Pints	100 min	11 lb	12 lb	13 lb	14 lb

Recommended process time for Fish in a weighted-gauge pressure canner

Style of Pack	Jar Size	Process Time	Canner Pressure (PSI) at Altitudes of	
			0– 1,000 ft	Above 1,000 ft
Raw	Pints	100 min	10 lb	15 lb

OYSTERS

Procedure: Keep live oysters on ice until ready to can. Wash shells. Heat 5 to 7 minutes in preheated oven at 400°F. Cool briefly in ice water. Drain, open shell, and remove meat. Wash meat in water containing 1/2 cup salt per gallon. Drain. Add 1/2 teaspoon salt to each pint, if desired. Fill half-pint or pint jars with meat and hot water, leaving 1-inch headspace. Adjust lids and process.

Recommended process time for Oysters in a dial-gauge pressure canner

Jar Size	Process Time	Canner Pressure (PSI) at Altitudes of			
		0– 2,000 ft	2,001– 4,000 ft	4,001– 6,000 ft	6,001– 8,000 ft
Half-pints or Pints	75 min	11 lb	12 lb	13 lb	14 lb

Recommended process time for Oysters in a weighted-gauge pressure canner

Jar Size	Process Time	Canner Pressure (PSI) at Altitudes of	
		0– 1,000 ft	Above 1,000 ft
Half-pints or Pints	75 min	10 lb	15 lb

SMOKED FISH

Salmon, rockfish and flatfish (sole, cod, flounder) and other fish.

Caution: Safe processing times for other smoked seafoods have not been determined. Those products should be frozen. Smoking of fish should be done by tested methods. Lightly smoked fish is recommended for canning. However, because it has not yet been cooked, do not taste lightly smoked fish before canning.

Follow these recommended canning instructions carefully. Use a 16 to 22 quart pressure canner for this procedure; do not use smaller pressure saucepans. Safe processing times haven't been determined. Do not use quart jars or tin cans. Half-pints could be safely processed for the same length of time as pints, but the quality of the product may be less acceptable.

Procedure: If smoked fish has been frozen, thaw in the refrigerator until no ice crystals remain before canning. If not done prior to smoking, cut fish into pieces that will fit vertically into pint canning jars, leaving 1-inch headspace. Measure 4 quarts (16 cups) of cool tap water and pour into the pressure canner. (**Note:** The water level probably will reach the screwbands of pints jars.) **Do not decrease the amount of water or heat the water before processing begins.** Pack smoked fish vertically into jars, leaving 1-inch headspace between the pieces and the top of the jar. The fish may be packed either loosely or tightly. Clean jar rims with a clean, damp paper towel. Do not add liquid to the jars. Adjust lids and process.

Recommended process time for Smoked Fish in a dial-gauge pressure canner

Jar Size	Process Time	Canner Pressure (PSI) at Altitudes of			
		0–2,000 ft	2,001–4,000 ft	4,001–6,000 ft	6,001–8,000 ft
Pints	110 min	11 lb	12 lb	13 lb	14 lb

Recommended process time for Smoked Fish in a weighted-gauge pressure canner

Jar Size	Process Time	Canner Pressure (PSI) at Altitudes of	
		0–1,000 ft	Above 1,000 ft
Pints	110 min	11 lb	15 lb

TUNA

Tuna may be canned either precooked or raw. Precooking removes most of the strong-flavored oils. The strong flavor of dark tuna flesh affects the delicate flavor of white flesh. Many people prefer not to can dark flesh. It may be used as pet food.

Note: Glass-like crystals of magnesium ammonium phosphate sometimes form in canned tuna. There is no way for the home canner to prevent these crystals from forming, but they usually dissolve when heated and are safe to eat.

Procedure: Keep tuna on ice until ready to can. Remove viscera and wash fish well in cold water. Allow blood to drain from stomach cavity. Place fish belly down on a rack or metal tray in the bottom of a large baking pan. Cut tuna in half crosswise, if necessary. Precook fish by baking at 250°F for 2-1/2 to 4 hours (depending on size) or at 350°F for 1 hour. The fish may also be cooked in a steamer for 2 to 4 hours. If a thermometer is used, cook to a 165° to 175°F internal temperature. Refrigerate cooked fish overnight to firm the meat. Peel off the skin with a knife, removing blood vessels and any discolored flesh. Cut meat away from bones; cut out and discard all bones, fin bases, and dark flesh. Quarter. Cut quarters crosswise into lengths suitable for half-pint or pint jars. Fill into jars, pressing down gently to make a solid pack. Tuna may be packed in water or oil, whichever is preferred. Add water or oil to jars, leaving 1-inch headspace. Add 1/2 teaspoon of salt per half-pint or 1 teaspoon of salt per pint, if desired. Adjust lids and process.

Recommended process time for Tuna in a dial-gauge pressure canner

Jar Size	Process Time	Canner Pressure (PSI) at Altitudes of			
		0–2,000 ft	2,001–4,000 ft	4,001–6,000 ft	6,001–8,000 ft
Half-pints or Pints	100 min	11 lb	12 lb	13 lb	14 lb

Recommended process time for Tuna in a weighted-gauge pressure canner

Jar Size	Process Time	Canner Pressure (PSI) at Altitudes of	
		0–1,000 ft	Above 1,000 ft
Half-pints or Pints	100 min	10 lb	15 lb

Complete Guide to Home Canning, Guide 6

PREPARING AND CANNING FERMENTED FOODS AND PICKLED VEGETABLES

Guide 6

Preparing and Canning Fermented Foods and Pickled Vegetables

Table of Contents, Guide 6
Preparing and Canning Fermented Foods and Pickled Vegetables

Selection of fresh cucumbers

Quantity: An average of 14 pounds is needed per canner load of 7 quarts; an average of 9 pounds is needed per canner load of 9 pints. A bushel weighs 48 pounds and yields 16 to 24 quarts—an average of 2 pounds per quart.

Quality: Select firm cucumbers of the appropriate size: about 1-1/2 inches for gherkins and 4 inches for dills. Use odd-shaped and more mature cucumbers for relishes and bread-and-butter style pickles.

Low-temperature pasteurization treatment

The following treatment results in a better product texture but must be carefully managed to avoid possible spoilage. Place jars in a canner filled half way with warm (120° to 140°F) water. Then, add hot water to a level 1 inch above jars. Heat the water enough to maintain 180° to 185°F water temperature for 30 minutes. Check with a candy or jelly thermometer to be certain that the water temperature is at least 180°F during the entire 30 minutes. Temperatures higher than 185°F may cause unnecessary softening of pickles. **Caution: Use only when recipe indicates.**

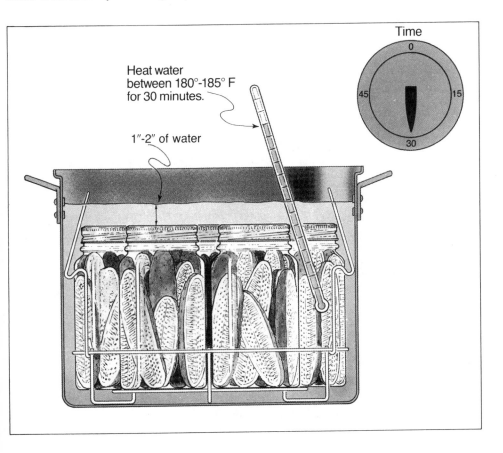

Heat water between 180°-185° F for 30 minutes.

1″-2″ of water

Time

Suitable containers, covers, and weights for fermenting food

A 1-gallon container is needed for each 5 pounds of fresh vegetables. Therefore, a 5-gallon stone crock is of ideal size for fermenting about 25 pounds of fresh cabbage or cucumbers. Food-grade plastic and glass containers are excellent substitutes for stone crocks. Other 1- to 3-gallon non-food-grade plastic containers may be used if lined inside with a clean food-grade plastic bag. **Caution: Be certain that foods contact only food-grade plastics. Do not use garbage bags or trash liners.** Fermenting sauerkraut in quart and half-gallon Mason jars is an acceptable practice, but may result in more spoilage losses.

Cabbage and cucumbers must be kept 1 to 2 inches under brine while fermenting. After adding prepared vegetables and brine, insert a suitably sized dinner plate or glass pie plate inside the fermentation container. The plate must be slightly smaller than the container opening, yet large enough to cover most of the shredded cabbage or cucumbers. To keep the plate under the brine, weight it down with 2 to 3 sealed quart jars filled with water. Covering the container opening with a clean, heavy bath towel helps to prevent contamination from insects and molds while the vegetables are fermenting. Fine quality fermented vegetables are also obtained when the plate is weighted down with a very large clean, plastic bag filled with 3 quarts of water containing 4-1/2 tablespoons of salt. Be sure to seal the plastic bag. Freezer bags sold for packaging turkeys are suitable for use with 5-gallon containers.

The fermentation container, plate, and jars must be washed in hot sudsy water, and rinsed well with very hot water before use.

Salts used in pickling

Use of canning or pickling salt is recommended. Fermented and nonfermented pickles may be safely made using either iodized or noniodized table salt. However, non-caking materials added to table salts may make the brine cloudy. Flake salt varies in density and is not recommended for use.

Reduced-sodium salts, for example "Lite Salt," may be used in quick pickle recipes, as indicated in this guide. The pickles may, however, have a slightly different taste than expected. **Caution: Use of reduced-sodium salt in fermented pickle recipes is not recommended.**

Fermented foods

DILL PICKLES

Use the following quantities for each gallon capacity of your container.

4 lbs of 4-inch pickling cucumbers
2 tbsp dill seed or 4 to 5 heads fresh or dry dill weed
1/2 cup salt
1/4 cup vinegar (5%)
8 cups water and one or more of the following ingredients:
    2 cloves garlic (optional)
    2 dried red peppers (optional)
    2 tsp whole mixed pickling spices (optional)

Procedure: Wash cucumbers. Cut 1/16-inch slice off blossom end and discard. Leave 1/4-inch of stem attached. Place half of dill and spices on bottom of a clean, suitable container (see page 6). Add cucumbers, remaining dill, and spices. Dissolve salt in vinegar and water and pour over cucumbers. Add suitable cover and weight. Store where temperature is between 70°F and 75°F for about 3 to 4 weeks while fermenting. Temperatures of 55° to 65°F are acceptable, but the fermentation will take 5 to 6 weeks. Avoid temperatures above 80°F, or pickles will become too soft during fermentation. Fermenting pickles cure slowly. Check the container several times a week and promptly remove surface scum or mold. **Caution: If the pickles become soft, slimy, or develop a disagreeable odor, discard them.** Fully fermented pickles may be stored in the original container for about 4 to 6 months, provided they are refrigerated and surface scum and molds are removed regularly. Canning fully fermented pickles is a better way to store them. To can them, pour the brine into a pan, heat slowly to a boil, and simmer 5 minutes. Filter brine through paper coffee filters to reduce cloudiness, if desired. Fill jar with pickles and hot brine, leaving 1/2-inch headspace. Adjust lids and process as below, or use the low-temperature pasteurization treatment described on page 5.

Recommended process time for Dill Pickles in a boiling-water canner

Style of Pack	Jar Size	Process Time at Altitudes of		
		0–1,000 ft	1,001–6,000 ft	Above 6,000 ft
Raw	Pints	10 min	15	20
	Quarts	15	20	25

SAUERKRAUT

25 lbs cabbage
3/4 cup canning or pickling salt

Quality: For the best sauerkraut, use firm heads of fresh cabbage. Shred cabbage and start kraut between 24 and 48 hours after harvest.

Yield: About 9 quarts

Procedure: Work with about 5 pounds of cabbage at a time. Discard outer leaves. Rinse heads under cold running water and drain. Cut heads in quarters and remove cores. Shred or slice to a thickness of a quarter. Put cabbage in a suitable fermentation container (see page 6), and add 3 tablespoons of salt. Mix thoroughly, using clean hands. Pack firmly until salt draws juices from cabbage. Repeat shredding, salting, and packing until all cabbage is in the container. Be sure it is deep enough so that its rim is at least 4 or 5 inches above the cabbage. If juice does not cover cabbage, add boiled and cooled brine (1-1/2 tablespoons of salt per quart of water). Add plate and weights; cover container with a clean bath towel. Store at 70° to 75°F while fermenting. At temperatures between 70° and 75°F, kraut will be fully fermented in about 3 to 4 weeks; at 60° to 65°F, fermentation may take 5 to 6 weeks. At temperatures lower than 60°F, kraut may not ferment. Above 75°F, kraut may become soft.

If you weigh the cabbage down with a brine-filled bag, do not disturb the crock until normal fermentation is completed (when bubbling ceases). If you use jars as weight, you will have to check the kraut 2 to 3 times each week and remove scum if it forms. Fully fermented kraut may be kept tightly covered in the refrigerator for several months or it may be canned as follows:

Hot pack—Bring kraut and liquid slowly to a boil in a large kettle, stirring frequently. Remove from heat and fill jars rather firmly with kraut and juices, leaving 1/2-inch headspace.

Raw pack—Fill jars firmly with kraut and cover with juices, leaving 1/2-inch headspace.

Adjust lids and process.

Recommended process time for Sauerkraut in a boiling-water canner

Style of Pack	Jar Size	Process Time at Altitudes of			
		0–1,000 ft	1,001–3,000 ft	3,001–6,000 ft	Above 6,000 ft
Hot	Pints	10 min	15	15	20
	Quarts	15	20	20	25
Raw	Pints	20	25	30	35
	Quarts	25	30	35	40

Pickled or nonfermented foods

PICKLED DILLED BEANS

4 lbs fresh tender green or yellow beans (5 to 6 inches long)
8 to 16 heads fresh dill
8 cloves garlic (optional)
1/2 cup canning or pickling salt
4 cups white vinegar (5%)
4 cups water
1 tsp hot red pepper flakes (optional)

Yield: About 8 pints

Procedure: Wash and trim ends from beans and cut to 4-inch lengths. In each sterile pint jar, place 1 to 2 dill heads and, if desired, 1 clove of garlic. Place whole beans upright in jars, leaving 1/2-inch headspace. Trim beans to ensure proper fit, if necessary. Combine salt, vinegar, water, and pepper flakes (if desired). Bring to a boil. Add hot solution to beans, leaving 1/2-inch headspace. Adjust lids and process.

Recommended process time for Pickled Dilled Beans in a boiling-water canner

Style of Pack	Jar Size	Process Time at Altitudes of		
		0– 1,000 ft	1,001– 6,000 ft	Above 6,000 ft
Raw	Pints	5 min	10	15

PICKLED THREE-BEAN SALAD

1-1/2 cups cut and blanched green or yellow beans (prepared as below)
1-1/2 cups canned, drained, red kidney beans
1 cup canned, drained garbanzo beans
1/2 cup peeled and thinly sliced onion (about 1 medium onion)
1/2 cup trimmed and thinly sliced celery (1-1/2 medium stalks)
1/2 cup sliced green peppers (1/2 medium pepper)
1/2 cup white vinegar (5%)
1/4 cup bottled lemon juice
3/4 cup sugar
1/4 cup oil
1/2 tsp canning or pickling salt
1-1/4 cups water

Yield: About 5 to 6 half-pints

Procedure: Wash and snap off ends of fresh beans. Cut or snap into 1- to 2-inch pieces. Blanch 3 minutes and cool immediately. Rinse kidney beans with tap water and drain again. Prepare and measure all other vegetables. Combine vinegar, lemon juice, sugar, and water and bring to a boil. Remove from heat. Add oil and salt and mix well. Add beans, onions, celery, and green pepper to solution and bring to a simmer. Marinate 12 to 14 hours in refrigerator, then heat entire mixture to a boil. Fill clean jars with solids. Add hot liquid, leaving 1/2-inch headspace. Adjust lids and process.

Recommended process time for Pickled Three-Bean Salad in a boiling-water canner

| Style of Pack | Jar Size | Process Time at Altitudes of | | |
		0–1,000 ft	1,001–6,000 ft	Above 6,000 ft
Hot	Half-pints or Pints	15 min	20	25

PICKLED BEETS

7 lbs of 2- to 2-1/2-inch diameter beets
4 cups vinegar (5%)
1-1/2 teaspoons canning or pickling salt
2 cups sugar
2 cups water
2 cinnamon sticks
12 whole cloves
4 to 6 onions (2- to 2-1/2-inch diameter), if desired

Yield: About 8 pints

Procedure: Trim off beet tops, leaving 1 inch of stem and roots to prevent bleeding of color. Wash thoroughly. Sort for size. Cover similar sizes together with boiling water and cook until tender (about 25 to 30 minutes). **Caution: Drain and discard liquid.** Cool beets. Trim off roots and stems and slip off skins. Slice into 1/4-inch slices. Peel and thinly slice onions. Combine vinegar, salt, sugar, and fresh water. Put spices in cheesecloth bag and add to vinegar mixture. Bring to a boil. Add beets and onions. Simmer 5 minutes. Remove spice bag. Fill jars with beets and onions, leaving 1/2-inch headspace. Add hot vinegar solution, allowing 1/2-inch headspace. Adjust lids and process.

Recommended process time for Pickled Beets in a boiling-water canner

Style of Pack	Jar Size	Process Time at Altitudes of			
		0–1,000 ft	1,001–3,000 ft	3,001–6,000 ft	Above 6,000 ft
Hot	Pints or Quarts	30 min	35	40	45

Variation: Pickled whole baby beets. Follow above directions but use beets that are 1- to 1-1/2 inches in diameter. Pack whole; do not slice. Onions may be omitted.

PICKLED CAULIFLOWER OR BRUSSEL SPROUTS

12 cups of 1- to 2-inch cauliflower flowerets or small brussel sprouts
4 cups white vinegar (5%)
2 cups sugar
2 cups thinly sliced onions
1 cup diced sweet red peppers
2 tbsp mustard seed
1 tbsp celery seed
1 tsp turmeric
1 tsp hot red pepper flakes

Yield: About 9 half-pints

Procedure: Wash cauliflower flowerets or brussel sprouts (remove stems and blemished outer leaves) and boil in salt water (4 tsp canning salt per gallon of water) for 3 minutes for cauliflower and 4 minutes for brussel sprouts. Drain and cool. Combine vinegar, sugar, onion, diced red pepper, and spices in large saucepan. Bring to a boil and simmer 5 minutes. Distribute onion and diced pepper among jars. Fill jars with pieces and pickling solution, leaving 1/2-inch headspace. Adjust lids and process.

Recommended process time for Pickled Cauliflower or Brussel Sprouts in a boiling-water canner

Style of Pack	Jar Size	Process Time at Altitudes of		
		0–1,000 ft	1,001–6,000 ft	Above 6,000 ft
Hot	Half-pints or Pints	10 min	15	20

PICKLED CORN RELISH

10 cups fresh whole kernel corn (16 to 20 medium-size ears), or
    six 10-ounce packages of frozen corn
2-1/2 cups diced sweet red peppers
2-1/2 cups diced sweet green peppers
2-1/2 cups chopped celery
1-1/4 cups diced onions
1-3/4 cups sugar
5 cups vinegar (5%)
2-1/2 tbsp canning or pickling salt
2-1/2 tsp celery seed
2-1/2 tbsp dry mustard
1-1/4 tsp turmeric

Yield: About 9 pints

Procedure: Boil ears of corn 5 minutes. Dip in cold water. Cut whole kernels from cob or use six 10-ounce frozen packages of corn. Combine peppers, celery, onions, sugar, vinegar, salt, and celery seed in a saucepan. Bring to boil and simmer 5 minutes, stirring occasionally. Mix mustard and turmeric in 1/2 cup of the simmered mixture. Add this mixture and corn to the hot mixture. Simmer another 5 minutes. If desired, thicken mixture with flour paste (1/4 cup flour blended in 1/4 cup water) and stir frequently. Fill jars with hot mixture, leaving 1/2-inch headspace. Adjust lids and process.

Recommended process time for Pickled Corn Relish in a boiling-water canner

Style of Pack	Jar Size	Process Time at Altitudes of		
		0– 1,000 ft	1,001– 6,000 ft	Above 6,000 ft
Hot	Half-pints or Pints	15 min	20	25

PICKLED HORSERADISH SAUCE

2 cups (3/4 lb) freshly grated horseradish
1 cup white vinegar (5%)
1/2 tsp canning or pickling salt
1/4 tsp powdered ascorbic acid

Yield: About 2 half-pints

Procedure: The pungency of fresh horseradish fades within 1 to 2 months, even when refrigerated. Therefore, make only small quantities at a time. Wash horseradish roots thoroughly and peel off brown outer skin. The peeled roots may be grated in a food processor or cut into small cubes and put through a food grinder. Combine ingredients and fill into sterile jars (see page 1·15), leaving 1/4-inch headspace. Seal jars tightly and store in a refrigerator.

MARINATED WHOLE MUSHROOMS

7 lbs small whole mushrooms
1/2 cup bottled lemon juice
2 cups olive or salad oil
2-1/2 cups white vinegar (5%)
1 tbsp oregano leaves
1 tbsp dried basil leaves
1 tbsp canning or pickling salt
1/2 cup finely chopped onions
1/4 cup diced pimiento
2 cloves garlic, cut in quarters
25 black peppercorns

Yield: About 9 half-pints

Procedure: Select very fresh unopened mushrooms with caps less than 1-1/4 inch in diameter. Wash. Cut stems, leaving 1/4 inch attached to cap. Add lemon juice and water to cover. Bring to boil. Simmer 5 minutes. Drain mushrooms. Mix olive oil, vinegar, oregano, basil, and salt in a saucepan. Stir in onions and pimiento and heat to boiling. Place 1/4 garlic clove and 2–3 peppercorns in a half-pint jar. Fill jars with mushrooms and hot, well-mixed oil/vinegar solution, leaving 1/2-inch headspace. Adjust lids and process.

Recommended process time for **Marinated Whole Mushrooms** in a boiling-water canner

Style of Pack	Jar Size	Process Time at Altitudes of			
		0–1,000 ft	1,001–3,000 ft	3,001–6,000 ft	Above 6,000 ft
Hot	Half-pints	20 min	25	30	35

PICKLED DILLED OKRA

7 lbs small okra pods
6 small hot peppers
4 tsp dill seed
8 to 9 garlic cloves
2/3 cup canning or pickling salt

6 cups water
6 cups vinegar (5%)

Yield: 8 to 9 pints

Procedure: Wash and trim okra. Fill jars firmly with whole okra, leaving 1/2-inch headspace. Place 1 garlic clove in each jar. Combine salt, hot peppers, dill seed, water, and vinegar in large saucepan and bring to a boil. Pour hot pickling solution over okra, leaving 1/2-inch headspace. Adjust lids and process.

Recommended process time for Pickled Dilled Okra in a boiling-water canner

Style of Pack	Jar Size	Process Time at Altitudes of		
		0–1,000 ft	1,001–6,000 ft	Above 6,000 ft
Hot	Pints	10 min	15	20

MARINATED PEPPERS

Bell, Hungarian, banana, or jalapeno

4 lbs firm peppers*
1 cup bottled lemon juice
2 cups white vinegar (5%)
1 tbsp oregano leaves
1 cup olive or salad oil
1/2 cup chopped onions
2 cloves garlic, quartered (optional)
2 tbsp prepared horseradish (optional)

*Note: It is possible to adjust the intensity of pickled jalapeno peppers by using all hot jalapeno peppers (hot style), or blending with sweet and mild peppers (medium or mild style).

For hot style: Use 4 lbs jalapeno peppers.

For medium style: Use 2 lbs jalapeno peppers and 2 lb sweet and mild peppers.

For mild style: Use 1 lb jalapeno peppers and 3 lbs sweet and mild peppers.

Yield: About 9 half-pints

Procedure: Select your favorite pepper. **Caution: If you select hot peppers, wear**

rubber or plastic gloves while handling them or wash hands thoroughly with soap and water before touching your face. Peppers may be left whole. Large peppers may be quartered. Wash, slash two to four slits in each pepper, and blanch in boiling water or blister in order to peel tough-skinned hot peppers.

Peppers may be blistered using one of the following methods: Oven or broiler method: Place peppers in a hot oven (400°F) or broiler for 6–8 minutes or until skins blister. Range-top method: Cover hot burner, either gas or electric, with heavy wire mesh. Place peppers on burner for several minutes until skins blister.

Allow peppers to cool. Place in pan and cover with a damp cloth. This will make peeling the peppers easier. After several minutes of cooling, peel each pepper. Flatten whole peppers. Mix all remaining ingredients in a saucepan and heat to boiling. Place 1/4 garlic clove (optional) and 1/4 teaspoon salt in each half pint or 1/2 teaspoon per pint. Fill jars with peppers, add hot, well-mixed oil/pickling solution over peppers, leaving 1/2-inch headspace. Adjust lids and process.

Recommended process time for Marinated Peppers in a boiling-water canner

Style of Pack	Jar Size	Process Time at Altitudes of			
		0– 1,000 ft	1,001– 3,000 ft	3,001– 6,000 ft	Above 6,000 ft
Raw	Half-pints or Pints	15 min	20	20	25

PICKLED BELL PEPPERS

7 lbs firm bell peppers
3-1/2 cups sugar
3 cups vinegar (5%)
3 cups water
9 cloves garlic
4-1/2 tsp canning or pickling salt

Yield: About 9 pints

Procedure: Wash peppers, cut into quarters, remove cores and seeds, and cut away any blemishes. Slice peppers in strips. Boil sugar, vinegar, and water for 1 minute. Add peppers and bring to a boil. Place 1/2 clove of garlic and 1/4 teaspoon salt in each sterile half-pint jar; double the amounts for pint jars. Add pepper strips and cover with hot vinegar mixture, leaving 1/2-inch headspace. Adjust lids and process.

Recommended process time for Pickled Bell Peppers in a boiling-water canner

Style of Pack	Jar Size	Process Time at Altitudes of		
		0– 1,000 ft	1,001– 6,000 ft	Above 6,000 ft
Hot	Half-pints or Pints	5 min	10	15

PICKLED HOT PEPPERS

Hungarian, banana, chile, jalapeno

4 lbs hot long red, green, or yellow peppers
3 lbs sweet red and green peppers, mixed
5 cups vinegar (5%)
1 cup water
4 tsp canning or pickling salt
2 tbsp sugar
2 cloves garlic

Yield: About 9 pints

Caution: Wear rubber gloves when handling hot peppers or wash hands thoroughly with soap and water before touching your face.

Procedure: Wash peppers. If small peppers are left whole, slash 2 to 4 slits in each. Quarter large peppers. Blanch in boiling water or blister in order to peel (see instructions for blistering for "Marinated Peppers," page 15). Cool and peel off skin. Flatten small peppers. Fill jars, leaving 1/2-inch headspace. Combine and heat other ingredients to boiling and simmer 10 minutes. Remove garlic. Add hot pickling solution over peppers, leaving 1/2-inch headspace. Adjust lids and process.

Recommended process time for Pickled Hot Peppers in a boiling-water canner

Style of Pack	Jar Size	Process Time at Altitudes of		
		0– 1,000 ft	1,001– 6,000 ft	Above 6,000 ft
Raw	Half-pints or Pints	10 min	15	20

PICKLED PEPPER-ONION RELISH

6 cups finely chopped onions
3 cups finely chopped sweet red peppers
3 cups finely chopped green peppers
1-1/2 cups sugar
6 cups vinegar (5%), preferably white distilled
2 tbsp canning or pickling salt

Yield: 9 half-pints

Procedure: Wash and chop vegetables. Combine all ingredients and boil gently until mixture thickens and volume is reduced by one-half (about 30 minutes). Fill sterile jars (see page 1·15) with hot relish, leaving 1/2-inch headspace, and seal tightly. Store in refrigerator and use within one month. **Caution: If extended storage is desired, this product must be processed.**

Recommended process time for Pickled Pepper-Onion Relish in a boiling-water canner

Style of Pack	Jar Size	Process Time at Altitudes of		
		0–1,000 ft	1,001–6,000 ft	Above 6,000 ft
Hot	Half-pints or Pints	5 min	10	15

PICCALILLI

6 cups chopped green tomatoes
1-1/2 cups chopped sweet red peppers
1-1/2 cups chopped green peppers
2-1/4 cups chopped onions
7-1/2 cups chopped cabbage
1/2 cup canning or pickling salt
3 tbsp whole mixed pickling spice
4-1/2 cups vinegar (5%)
3 cups brown sugar

Yield: 9 half-pints

Procedure: Wash, chop, and combine vegetables with 1/2 cup salt. Cover with hot water and let stand 12 hours. Drain and press in a clean white cloth to remove all possible liquid. Tie spices loosely in a spice bag and add to combined vinegar and brown sugar, and heat to a boil in a saucepan. Add vegetables and boil gently 30 minutes or until the volume of the mixture is reduced by one-half. Remove spice bag. Fill hot sterile jars (see page 1-15) with hot mixture, leaving 1/2-inch headspace. Adjust lids and process.

Recommended process time for **Piccalilli** in a boiling-water canner

Style of Pack	Jar Size	Process Time at Altitudes of		
		0–1,000 ft	1,001–6,000 ft	Above 6,000 ft
Hot	Half-pints or Pints	5 min	10	15

BREAD-AND-BUTTER PICKLES

6 lbs of 4- to 5-inch pickling cucumbers
8 cups thinly sliced onions (about 3 pounds)
1/2 cup canning or pickling salt
4 cups vinegar (5%)
4-1/2 cups sugar
2 tbsp mustard seed
1-1/2 tbsp celery seed
1 tbsp ground turmeric
1 cup pickling lime (optional—for use in variation below to make firmer pickles)

Yield: About 8 pints

Procedure: Wash cucumbers. Cut 1/16-inch off blossom end and discard. Cut into 3/16-inch slices. Combine cucumbers and onions in a large bowl. Add salt. Cover with 2 inches crushed or cubed ice. Refrigerate 3 to 4 hours, adding more ice as needed.

Combine remaining ingredients in a large pot. Boil 10 minutes. Drain and add cucumbers and onions and slowly reheat to boiling. Fill jars with slices and cooking syrup, leaving 1/2-inch headspace. Adjust lids and process as below or use low-temperature pasteurization treatment described on page 5.

Variation for firmer pickles: Wash cucumbers. Cut 1/16-inch off blossom end and discard. Cut into 3/16-inch slices. Mix 1 cup pickling lime and 1/2 cup salt to 1 gallon water in a 2- to 3-gallon crock or enamelware container. Avoid inhaling lime dust while mixing the lime-water solution. Soak cucumber slices in lime water for 12 to 24 hours, stirring occasionally. Remove from lime solution, rinse, and resoak 1 hour in fresh cold water. Repeat the rinsing and soaking steps two more times. Handle carefully, as slices will be brittle. Drain well.

Recommended process time for **Bread-and-Butter Pickles** in a boiling-water canner

Style of Pack	Jar Size	Process Time at Altitudes of		
		0–1,000 ft	1,001–6,000 ft	Above 6,000 ft
Hot	Pints or Quarts	10 min	15	20

Storage: After processing and cooling, jars should be stored 4 to 5 weeks to develop ideal flavor.

Variation: Squash bread-and-butter pickles. Substitute slender (1 to 1-1/2 inches in diameter) zucchini or yellow summer squash for cucumbers.

QUICK FRESH-PACK DILL PICKLES

8 lbs of 3- to 5-inch pickling cucumbers
2 gals water
1-1/4 cups canning or pickling salt (divided)
1-1/2 qts vinegar (5%)
1/4 cup sugar
2 qts water
2 tbsp whole mixed pickling spice
about 3 tbsp whole mustard seed (1 tsp per pint jar)
about 14 heads of fresh dill (1-1/2 heads per pint jar) or
    4-1/2 tbsp dill seed (1-1/2 tsp per pint jar)

Yield: 7 to 9 pints

Procedure: Wash cucumbers. Cut 1/16-inch slice off blossom end and discard, but leave 1/4-inch stem attached. Dissolve 3/4 cup salt in 2 gals water. Pour over cucumbers and let stand 12 hours. Drain. Combine vinegar, 1/2 cup salt, sugar, and 2 quarts water. Add mixed pickling spices tied in a clean white cloth. Heat to boiling. Fill jars with cucumbers. Add 1 tsp mustard seed and 1-1/2 heads fresh dill per pint. Cover with boiling pickling solution, leaving 1/2-inch headspace. Adjust lids and process as below or use the low-temperature pasteurization treatment described on page 5.

Recommended process time for Quick Fresh-Pack Dill Pickles in a bolling-water canner

Style of Pack	Jar Size	Process Time at Altitudes of		
		0–1,000 ft	1,001–6,000 ft	Above 6,000 ft
Raw	Pints	10 min	15	20
	Quarts	15	20	25

REDUCED-SODIUM SLICED DILL PICKLES

4 lbs (3- to 5-inch) pickling cucumbers
6 cups vinegar (5%)
6 cups sugar

2 tbsp canning or pickling salt
1-1/2 tsp celery seed
1-1/2 tsp mustard seed
2 large onions, thinly sliced
8 heads fresh dill

Yield: About 8 pints

Procedure: Wash cucumbers. Cut 1/16-inch slice off blossom end and discard. Cut cucumbers in 1/4-inch slices. Combine vinegar, sugar, salt, celery, and mustard seeds in large saucepan. Bring mixture to boiling. Place 2 slices of onion and 1/2 dill head on bottom of each pint jar. Fill jars with cucumber slices, leaving 1/2-inch headspace. Add 1 slice of onion and 1/2 dill head on top. Pour hot pickling solution over cucumbers, leaving 1/4-inch headspace. Adjust lids and process.

Recommended process time for Reduced-Sodium Sliced Dill Pickles in a boiling-water canner

Style of Pack	Jar Size	Process Time at Altitudes of		
		0–1,000 ft	1,001–6,000 ft	Above 6,000 ft
Raw	Pints	15 min	20	25

SWEET GHERKIN PICKLES

7 lbs cucumbers (1-1/2 inch or less)
1/2 cup canning or pickling salt
8 cups sugar
6 cups vinegar (5%)
3/4 tsp turmeric
2 tsp celery seeds
2 tsp whole mixed pickling spice
2 cinnamon sticks
1/2 tsp fennel (optional)
2 tsp vanilla (optional)

Yield: 6 to 7 pints

Procedure: Wash cucumbers. Cut 1/16-inch slice off blossom end and discard, but leave 1/4-inch of stem attached. Place cucumbers in large container and cover with boiling water. Six to 8 hours later, and on the second day, drain and cover with 6 quarts of fresh boiling water containing 1/4-cup salt. On the third day, drain and prick cucumbers with a table fork. Combine and bring to boil 3 cups vinegar, 3 cups sugar, turmeric, and spices. Pour over cucumbers. Six to 8 hours later, drain and save the pickling syrup. Add another 2 cups each of sugar and vinegar and reheat to boil. Pour over pickles. On the fourth day, drain and save syrup. Add another 2 cups sugar and 1 cup vinegar. Heat to boiling and pour over pickles. Drain and save pickling syrup 6 to 8 hours later. Add 1 cup sugar and 2 tsp vanilla and heat to boiling. Fill sterile pint jars (see page 1·15) with pickles and cover with hot syrup, leaving 1/2-inch headspace. Adjust lids and process as below, or use the low-temperature pasteurization treatment described on page 5.

Recommended process time for Sweet Gherkin Pickles in a boiling-water canner

Style of Pack	Jar Size	Process Time at Altitudes of		
		0–1,000 ft	1,001–6,000 ft	Above 6,000 ft
Raw	Pints	5 min	10	15

PICKLE RELISH

3 qts chopped cucumbers
3 cups each of chopped sweet green and red peppers
1 cup chopped onions
3/4 cup canning or pickling salt
4 cups ice
8 cups water
2 cups sugar
4 tsp each of mustard seed, turmeric, whole allspice, and whole cloves
6 cups white vinegar (5%)

Yield: About 9 pints

Procedure: Add cucumbers, peppers, onions, salt, and ice to water and let stand 4 hours. Drain and re-cover vegetables with fresh ice water for another hour. Drain again. Combine spices in a spice or cheesecloth bag. Add spices to sugar and vinegar. Heat to boiling and pour mixture over vegetables. Cover and refrigerate 24 hours. Heat mixture to boiling and fill hot into clean jars, leaving 1/2-inch headspace. Adjust lids and process.

Recommended process time for Pickle Relish in a boiling-water canner

Style of Pack	Jar Size	Process Time at Altitudes of		
		0–1,000 ft	1,001–6,000 ft	Above 6,000 ft
Hot	Half-pints or Pints	10 min	15	20

14-DAY SWEET PICKLES

Can be canned whole, in strips, or in slices

4 lbs of 2- to 5-inch pickling cucumbers
  (If packed whole, use cucumbers of uniform size)
3/4 cup canning or pickling salt
  (Separated—1/4 cup on each of the 1st, 3rd, and 5th days)
2 tsp celery seed
2 tbsp mixed pickling spices
5-1/2 cups sugar
4 cups vinegar (5%)

Yield: About 5 to 9 pints

Procedure: Wash cucumbers. Cut 1/16-inch slice off blossom end and discard, but leave 1/4-inch of stem attached. Place whole cucumbers in suitable 1-gallon container (see page 6). Add 1/4 cup canning or pickling salt to 2 quarts water and bring to a boil. Pour over cucumbers. Add suitable cover and weight. Place clean towel over container and keep the temperature at about 70°F. **On the third and fifth days,** drain salt water and discard. Rinse cucumbers and rescald cover and weight. Return cucumbers to container. Add 1/4 cup salt to 2 quarts fresh water and boil. Pour over cucumbers. Replace cover and weight, and re-cover with clean towel. On the seventh day, drain salt water and discard. Rinse cucumbers and rescald containers, cover, and weight. Slice or strip cucumbers, if desired, and return to container. Place celery seed and pickling spices in small cheesecloth bag. Combine 2 cups sugar and 4 cups vinegar in a saucepan. Add spice bag, bring to a boil and pour pickling solution over cucumbers. Add cover and weight, and re-cover with clean towel. **On each of the next six days,** drain syrup and spice bag and save. Add 1/2 cup sugar each day and bring to a boil in a saucepan. Remove cucumbers and rinse. Scald container, cover, and weight daily. Return cucumbers to container, add boiled syrup, cover, weight, and re-cover with towel. **On the 14th day,** drain syrup into saucepan. Fill sterile pint jars (see page 1·15) or clean quart jars, leaving 1/2-inch headspace. Add 1/2 cup sugar to syrup and bring to boil. Remove spice bag. Pour hot syrup over cucumbers, leaving 1/2-inch headspace. Adjust lids and process as below or use low-temperature pasteurization treatment described on page 5.

Recommended process time for 14-Day Sweet Pickles in a boiling-water canner

Style of Pack	Jar Size	Process Time at Altitudes of		
		0–1,000 ft	1,001–6,000 ft	Above 6,000 ft
Raw	Pints	5 min	10	15
	Quarts	10	15	20

QUICK SWEET PICKLES

May be canned as either strips or slices.

8 lbs of 3- to 4-inch pickling cucumbers
1/3 cup canning or pickling salt
4-1/2 cups sugar
3-1/2 cups vinegar (5%)
2 tsp celery seed
1 tbsp whole allspice
2 tbsp mustard seed
1 cup pickling lime (optional—for use in variation below to make firmer pickles)

Yield: About 7 to 9 pints

Procedure: Wash cucumbers. Cut 1/16-inch off blossom end and discard, but leave 1/4 inch of stem attached. Slice or cut in strips, if desired. Place in bowl and sprinkle with 1/3 cup salt. Cover with 2 inches of crushed or cubed ice. Refrigerate 3 to 4 hours. Add more ice as needed. Drain well.

Combine sugar, vinegar, celery seed, allspice, and mustard seed in 6-quart kettle. Heat to boiling.

Hot pack—Add cucumbers and heat slowly until vinegar solution returns to boil. Stir occasionally to make sure mixture heats evenly. Fill sterile jars, leaving 1/2-inch headspace.

Raw pack—Fill jars, leaving 1/2-inch headspace. Add hot pickling syrup, leaving 1/2-inch headspace. Adjust lids and process as below or use the low temperature pasteurization treatment described on page 5.

Variation for firmer pickles: Wash cucumbers. Cut 1/16-inch off blossom end and discard, but leave 1/4-inch of stem attached. Slice or strip cucumbers. Mix 1 cup pickling lime and 1/2 cup salt to 1 gallon water in a 2- to 3-gallon crock or enamelware container. **Caution: Avoid inhaling lime dust while mixing the lime-water solution.** Soak cucumber slices or strips in lime water solution for 12 to 24 hours, stirring occasionally. Remove from lime solution and rinse and resoak 1 hour in fresh cold water. Repeat the rinsing and resoaking two more times. Handle carefully because slices or strips will be brittle. Drain well.

Recommended process time for Quick Sweet Pickles in a boiling-water canner

Style of Pack	Jar Size	Process Time at Altitudes of		
		0–1,000 ft	1,001–6,000 ft	Above 6,000 ft
Hot	Pints or Quarts	5 min	10	15
Raw	Pints	10	15	20
	Quarts	15	20	25

Storage: After processing and cooling, jars should be stored 4 to 5 weeks to develop ideal flavor.

Variation: Add 2 slices of raw whole onion to each jar before filling with cucumbers.

REDUCED-SODIUM SLICED SWEET PICKLES

4 lbs (3- to 4-inch) pickling cucumbers

Brining solution:
1 qt distilled white vinegar (5%)
1 tbsp canning or pickling salt
1 tbsp mustard seed
1/2 cup sugar

Canning syrup:
1-2/3 cups distilled white vinegar (5%)
3 cups sugar
1 tbsp whole allspice
2-1/4 tsp celery seed

Yield: About 4 to 5 pints

Procedure: Wash cucumbers and cut 1/16 inch off blossom end, and discard. Cut cucumbers into 1/4-inch slices. Combine all ingredients for canning syrup in a saucepan and bring to boiling. Keep syrup hot until used. In a large kettle, mix the ingredients for the brining solution. Add the cut cucumbers, cover, and simmer until the cucumbers change color from bright to dull green (about 5 to 7 minutes). Drain the cucumber slices. Fill jars, and cover with hot canning syrup leaving 1/2-inch headspace. Adjust lids and process.

Recommended process time for Reduced-Sodium Sliced Sweet Pickles in a boiling-water canner

Style of Pack	Jar Size	Process Time at Altitudes of		
		0– 1,000 ft	1,001– 6,000 ft	Above 6,000 ft
Hot	Pints	10 min	15	20

PICKLED SWEET GREEN TOMATOES

10 to 11 lbs of green tomatoes (16 cups sliced)
2 cups sliced onions
1/4 cup canning or pickling salt
3 cups brown sugar
4 cups vinegar (5%)
1 tbsp mustard seed
1 tbsp allspice
1 tbsp celery seed
1 tbsp whole cloves

Yield: About 9 pints

Procedure: Wash and slice tomatoes and onions. Place in bowl, sprinkle with 1/4 cup salt, and let stand 4 to 6 hours. Drain. Heat and stir sugar in vinegar until dissolved. Tie mustard seed, allspice, celery seed, and cloves in a spice bag. Add to vinegar with tomatoes and onions. If needed, add minimum water to cover pieces. Bring to boil and simmer 30 minutes, stirring as needed to prevent burning. Tomatoes should be tender and transparent when properly cooked. Remove spice bag. Fill jar and cover with hot pickling solution, leaving 1/2-inch headspace. Adjust lids and process.

Recommended process time for Pickled Sweet Green Tomatoes in a boiling-water canner

Style of Pack	Jar Size	Process Time at Altitudes of		
		0– 1,000 ft	1,001– 6,000 ft	Above 6,000 ft
Hot	Pints	10 min	15	20
	Quarts	15	20	25

PICKLED GREEN TOMATO RELISH

10 lbs small, hard green tomatoes
1-1/2 lbs red bell peppers
1-1/2 lbs green bell peppers
2 lbs onions

1/2 cup canning or pickling salt
1 qt water
4 cups sugar
1 qt vinegar (5%)
1/3 cup prepared yellow mustard
2 tbsp cornstarch

Yield: 7 to 9 pints

Procedure: Wash and coarsely grate or finely chop tomatoes, peppers, and onions. Dissolve salt in water and pour over vegetables in large kettle. Heat to boiling and simmer 5 minutes. Drain in colander. Return vegetables to kettle. Add sugar, vinegar, mustard, and cornstarch. Stir to mix. Heat to boil and simmer 5 minutes. Fill sterile pint jars (see page 1·15) with hot relish, leaving 1/2-inch headspace. Adjust lids and process.

Recommended process time for Pickled Green Tomato Relish in a boiling-water canner

Style of Pack	Jar Size	Process Time at Altitudes of		
		0–1,000 ft	1,001–6,000 ft	Above 6,000 ft
Hot	Pints	5 min	10	15

PICKLED MIXED VEGETABLES

4 lbs of 4- to 5-inch pickling cucumbers, washed, and cut into 1-inch slices (cut off
  1/16 inch from blossom end and discard)
2 lbs peeled and quartered small onions
4 cups cut celery (1-inch pieces)
2 cups peeled and cut carrots (1/2-inch pieces)
2 cups cut sweet red peppers (1/2-inch pieces)
2 cups cauliflower flowerets
5 cups white vinegar (5%)
1/4 cup prepared mustard
1/2 cup canning or pickling salt
3-1/2 cups sugar
3 tbsp celery seed
2 tbsp mustard seed
1/2 tsp whole cloves
1/2 tsp ground turmeric

Yield: About 10 pints

Procedure: Combine vegetables, cover with 2 inches of cubed or crushed ice, and refrigerate 3 to 4 hours. In 8-quart kettle, combine vinegar and mustard and mix well. Add salt, sugar, celery seed, mustard seed, cloves, turmeric. Bring to a boil. Drain vegetables and add to hot pickling solution. Cover and slowly bring to boil. Drain vegetables but save pickling solution. Fill vegetables in sterile pint jars, or clean quarts, leaving 1/2-inch headspace. Add pickling solution, leaving 1/2-inch headspace. Adjust lids and process.

Recommended process time for Pickled Mixed Vegetables in a boiling-water canner

Style of Pack	Jar Size	Process Time at Altitudes of		
		0–1,000 ft	1,001–6,000 ft	Above 6,000 ft
Hot	Pints	5 min	10	15
	Quarts	10	15	20

PICKLED BREAD-AND-BUTTER ZUCCHINI

16 cups fresh zucchini, sliced
4 cups onions, thinly sliced
1/2 cup canning or pickling salt
4 cups white vinegar (5%)
2 cups sugar
4 tbsp mustard seed
2 tbsp celery seed
2 tsp ground turmeric

Yield: About 8 to 9 pints

Procedure: Cover zucchini and onion slices with 1 inch of water and salt. Let stand 2 hours and drain thoroughly. Combine vinegar, sugar, and spices. Bring to a boil and add zucchini and onions. Simmer 5 minutes and fill jars with mixture and pickling solution, leaving 1/2-inch headspace. Adjust lids and process or use low-temperature pasteurization treatment described on page 5.

Recommended process time for Pickled Bread and Butter Zucchini in a boiling-water canner

Style of Pack	Jar Size	Process Time at Altitudes of		
		0–1,000 ft	1,001–6,000 ft	Above 6,000 ft
Hot	Pints or Quarts	10 min	15	20

PREPARING AND CANNING JAMS AND JELLIES

Guide 7

Preparing and Canning Jams and Jellies

Table of Contents, Guide 7

Preparing and Canning Jams and Jellies

Making jelly without added pectin

Use only firm fruits naturally high in pectin. Select a mixture of about 3/4 ripe and 1/4 underripe fruit. Do not use commercially canned or frozen fruit juices. Their pectin content is too low. Wash all fruits thoroughly before cooking. Crush soft fruits or berries; cut firmer fruits into small pieces. Using the peels and cores adds pectin to the juice during cooking. Add water to fruits that require it, as listed in the table of ingredients below. Put fruit and water in large saucepan and bring to a boil. Then simmer according to the times below until fruit is soft, while stirring to prevent scorching. One pound of fruit should yield at least 1 cup of clear juice.

Extracting juices and making jelly

To Extract Juice

	Cups of Water to be Added per Pound of Fruit	Minutes to Simmer Fruit before Extracting Juice	Ingredients Added to Each Cup of Strained Juice		Yield from 4 Cups of Juice (Half-pints)
			Sugar (Cups)	Lemon Juice (Tsp)	
Apples	1	20 to 25	3/4	1-1/2 (opt)	4 to 5
Blackberries	None or 1/4	5 to 10	3/4 to 1	None	7 to 8
Crab apples	1	20 to 25	1	None	4 to 5
Grapes	None or 1/4	5 to 10	3/4 to 1	None	8 to 9
Plums	1/2	15 to 20	3/4	None	8 to 9

When fruit is tender, strain through a colander, then strain through a double layer of cheesecloth or a jelly bag. Allow juice to drip through, using a stand or colander to hold the bag. Pressing or squeezing the bag or cloth will cause cloudy jelly.

Using no more than 6 to 8 cups of extracted fruit juice at a time, measure fruit juice, sugar, and lemon juice according to the ingredients in the table above and heat to boiling. Stir until the sugar is dissolved. Boil over high heat to the jellying point. To test jelly for doneness, use one of the following methods.

Temperature test: Use a jelly or candy thermometer and boil until mixture reaches the following temperatures at altitudes of:

Sea Level	1,000 ft	2,000 ft	3,000 ft	4,000 ft	5,000 ft	6,000 ft	7,000 ft	8,000 ft
220°F	218°F	216°F	214°F	212°F	211°F	209°F	207°F	205°F

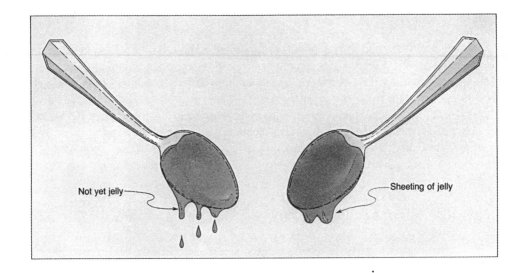

Not yet jelly

Sheeting of jelly

Sheet or spoon test—Dip a cool metal spoon into the boiling jelly mixture. Raise the spoon about 12 inches above the pan (out of steam). Turn the spoon so the liquid runs off the side. The jelly is done when the syrup forms two drops that flow together and sheet or hang off the edge of the spoon.

Remove from heat and quickly skim off foam. Fill sterile jars (see page 1·15) with jelly. Use a measuring cup or ladle the jelly through a wide-mouthed funnel, leaving 1/4-inch headspace. Adjust lids and process.

Recommended process time for Jelly without Added Pectin in a boiling-water canner

Style of Pack	Jar Size	Process Time at Altitudes of		
		0–1,000 ft	1,001–6,000 ft	Above 6,000 ft
Hot	Half-pints or Pints	5 min	10	15

Making jam without added pectin

Wash and rinse all fruits thoroughly before cooking. Do not soak. For best flavor, use fully ripe fruit. Remove stems, skins, and pits from fruit; cut into pieces and crush. For berries, remove stems and blossoms and crush. Seedy berries may be put through a sieve or food mill. Measure crushed fruit into large saucepan using the ingredient quantities specified in the table below.

Ingredient Quantities

Fruit	Cups Crushed Fruit	Cups Sugar	Tbsp Lemon Juice	Yield (Half-pints)
Apricots	4 to 4-1/2	4	2	5 to 6
Berries*	4	4	0	3 to 4
Peaches	5-1/2 to 6	4 to 5	2	6 to 7

*Includes blackberries, boysenberries, dewberries, gooseberries, loganberries, raspberries, and strawberries.

Add sugar and bring to a boil while stirring rapidly and constantly. Continue to boil until mixture thickens. Use one of the following tests to determine when jams and jellies are ready to fill. Remember to allow for thickening during cooling.

Temperature test—Use a jelly or candy thermometer and boil until mixture reaches the temperature for your altitude (see page 5).

Refrigerator test—Remove the jam mixture from the heat. Pour a small amount of boiling jam on a cold plate and put it in the freezing compartment of a refrigerator for a few minutes. If the mixture gels, it is ready to fill.

Remove from heat and skim off foam quickly. Fill sterile jars (see page 1·15) with jam. Use a measuring cup or ladle the jam through a wide-mouthed funnel, leaving 1/4-inch headspace. Adjust lids and process.

Recommended process time for Jams without Added Pectin in a boiling-water canner

Style of Pack	Jar Size	Process Time at Altitudes of		
		0–1,000 ft	1,001–6,000 ft	Above 6,000 ft
Hot	Half-pints or Pints	5 min	10	15

Making jams and jellies with added pectin

Fresh fruits and juices as well as commercially canned or frozen fruit juice can be used with commercially prepared powdered or liquid pectins. The order of combining ingredients depends on the type of pectin used. Complete directions for a variety of fruits are provided with packaged pectin. Jelly or jam made with added pectin requires less cooking and generally gives a larger yield. These products have more natural fruit flavors, too. In addition, using added pectin eliminates the need to test hot jellies and jams for proper gelling. Adding 1/2 teaspoon of butter or margarine with the juice and pectin will reduce foaming. However, these may cause off-flavor in long-term storage of jellies and jams. Recipes available using packaged pectin include:

Jellies—Apple, crab apple, blackberry, boysenberry, dewberry, currant, elderberry, grape, mayhaw, mint, peach, plum, black or red raspberry, loganberry, rhubarb, and strawberry.

Jams—Apricot, blackberry, boysenberry, dewberry, loganberry, red raspberry, youngberry, blueberry, cherry, currant, fig, gooseberry, grape, orange marmalade, peach, pear, plum, rhubarb, strawberry, and spiced tomato.

Be sure to use Mason canning jars, self-sealing two-piece lids, and a 5-minute process (corrected for altitude, as necessary) in boiling water. (see page 1·32) about spoilage of jams and jellies.)

Purchase fresh pectin each year. Old pectin may result in poor gels. Follow the instructions with each package and process as below:

Recommended process time for Jellies and Jam with Added Pectin in a boiling-water canner

Style of Pack	Jar Size	Process Time at Altitudes of		
		0– 1,000 ft	1,001– 6,000 ft	Above 6,000 ft
Hot	Half-pints or Pints	5 min	10	15

Following are a few additional jelly and jam recipes for use with packaged pectin.

PEAR-APPLE JAM

2 cups peeled, cored, and finely chopped pears (about 2 lbs)
1 cup peeled, cored, and finely chopped apples
6-1/2 cups sugar
1/4 tsp ground cinnamon
1/3 cup bottled lemon juice
6 oz liquid pectin

Yield: About 7 to 8 half-pints

Procedure: Crush apples and pears in a large saucepan and stir in cinnamon. Thoroughly mix sugar and lemon juice with fruits and bring to a boil over high heat, stirring constantly. Immediately stir in pectin. Bring to a full rolling boil and boil hard 1 minute, stirring constantly. Remove from heat, quickly skim off foam, and fill sterile jars (see page 1·15) leaving 1/4-inch headspace. Adjust lids and process.

Recommended process time for Pear-Apple Jam in a boiling-water canner

Style of Pack	Jar Size	Process Time at Altitudes of		
		0–1,000 ft	1,001–6,000 ft	Above 6,000 ft
Hot	Half-pints or Pints	5 min	10	15

STRAWBERRY-RHUBARB JELLY

1-1/2 lbs red stalks of rhubarb
1-1/2 qts ripe strawberries
1/2 tsp butter or margarine to reduce foaming (optional)
6 cups sugar
6 oz liquid pectin

Yield: About 7 half-pints

Procedure: Wash and cut rhubarb into 1-inch pieces and blend or grind. Wash, stem, and crush strawberries, one layer at a time, in a saucepan. Place both fruits in a jelly bag or double layer of cheesecloth and gently squeeze out juice. Measure 3-1/2 cups of juice into a large saucepan. Add butter and sugar, thoroughly mixing into juice. Bring to a boil over high heat, stirring constantly. Immediately stir in pectin. Bring to a full rolling boil and boil hard 1 minute, stirring constantly. Remove from heat, quickly skim off foam, and fill sterile jars (see page 1·15), leaving 1/4-inch headspace. Adjust lids and process.

Recommended process time for Strawberry-Rhubarb Jelly in a boiling-water canner

Style of Pack	Jar Size	Process Time at Altitudes of		
		0–1,000 ft	1,001–6,000 ft	Above 6,000 ft
Hot	Half-pints or Pints	5 min	10	15

BLUEBERRY-SPICE JAM

2-1/2 pints ripe blueberries
1 tbsp lemon juice
1/2 tsp ground nutmeg or cinnamon
5-1/2 cups sugar
3/4 cup water
1 box (1-3/4 oz) powdered pectin

Yield: About 5 half-pints

Procedure: Wash and thoroughly crush blueberries, one layer at a time, in a saucepan. Add lemon juice, spice, and water. Stir in pectin and bring to a full rolling boil over high heat, stirring frequently. Add the sugar and return to a full rolling boil. Boil hard for 1 minute, stirring constantly. Remove from heat, quickly skim off foam, and fill sterile jars (see page 1·15), leaving 1/4-inch headspace. Adjust lids and process.

Recommended process time for Blueberry-Spice Jam in a boiling-water canner

Style of Pack	Jar Size	Process Time at Altitudes of		
		0– 1,000 ft	1,001– 6,000 ft	Above 6,000 ft
Hot	Half-pints or Pints	5 min	10	15

GRAPE-PLUM JELLY

3-1/2 lbs ripe plums
3 lbs ripe Concord grapes
1 cup water
1/2 tsp butter or margarine to reduce foaming (optional)
8-1/2 cups sugar
1 box (1-3/4 oz) powdered pectin

Yield: About 10 half-pints

Procedure: Wash and pit plums; do not peel. Thoroughly crush the plums and grapes, one layer at a time, in a saucepan with water. Bring to a boil, cover, and simmer 10 minutes. Strain juice through a jelly bag or double layer of cheesecloth. Measure sugar and set aside. Combine 6-1/2 cups of juice with butter and pectin in large saucepan. Bring to a hard boil over high heat, stirring constantly. Add the sugar and return to a full rolling boil. Boil hard for 1 minute, stirring constantly. Remove from heat, quickly skim off foam, and fill sterile jars (see page 1·15), leaving 1/4-inch headspace. Adjust lids and process.

Recommended process time for Grape-Plum Jelly in a boiling-water canner

Style of Pack	Jar Size	Process Time at Altitudes of		
		0– 1,000 ft	1,001– 6,000 ft	Above 6,000 ft
Hot	Half-pints or Pints	5 min	10	15

Making reduced-sugar fruit spreads

A variety of fruit spreads may be made that are tasteful, yet lower in sugars and calories than regular jams and jellies. The following are recipes for reduced-sugar fruit spreads. Gelatin may be used as a thickening agent, as indicated in two of the following recipes. Sweet fruits, apple juice, spices, and/or a liquid, low-calorie sweetener are used to provide the sweet flavor of the fruit spreads. When gelatin is used in the recipe, the jars of spread should not be processed. They should be refrigerated and used within 4 weeks.

PEACH-PINEAPPLE SPREAD

4 cups drained peach pulp (procedure as below)
2 cups drained unsweetened crushed pineapple
1/4 cup bottled lemon juice
2 cups sugar (optional)

This recipe may be made with any combination of peaches, nectarines, apricots, and plums.

This recipe may be made without sugar or with up to 2 cups, according to taste or preference. Nonnutritive sweeteners may be added. If aspartame (a low-calorie nutritive sweetener) is used, the sweetening power of aspartame may be lost within 3 to 4 weeks.

Yield: 5 to 6 half-pints

Procedure: Thoroughly wash 4 to 6 pounds of firm, ripe peaches. Drain well. Peel and remove pits. Grind fruit flesh with a medium or coarse blade, or crush with a fork (do not use a blender). Place ground or crushed fruit in a 2-quart saucepan. Heat slowly to release juice, stirring constantly, until fruit is tender. Place cooked fruit in a jelly bag or strainer lined with four layers of cheesecloth. Allow juice to drip about 15 minutes. Save the juice for jelly or other uses. Measure 4 cups of drained fruit pulp for making spread. Combine the 4 cups of pulp, pineapple, and lemon juice in a 4-quart saucepan. Add up to 2 cups of sugar, if desired, and mix well. Heat and boil gently for 10 to 15 minutes, stirring enough to prevent sticking. Fill jars quickly, leaving 1/4-inch headspace. Adjust lids and process.

Recommended process time for Peach-Pineapple Spread in a boiling-water canner

Style of Pack	Jar Size	Process Time at Altitudes of			
		0–1,000 ft	1,001–3,000 ft	3,001–6,000 ft	Above 6,000 ft
Hot	Half-pints	15 min	20	20	25
	Pints	20	25	30	35

REFRIGERATED APPLE SPREAD (made with gelatin)

2 tbsp unflavored gelatin powder
1 qt bottle unsweetened apple juice
2 tbsp bottled lemon juice
2 tbsp liquid low-calorie sweetener
Food coloring, if desired

Yield: 4 half-pints

Procedure: In a saucepan, soften the gelatin in the apple and lemon juices. To dissolve gelatin, bring to a full rolling boil and boil 2 minutes. Remove from heat. Stir in sweetener and food coloring, if desired. Fill jars, leaving 1/4-inch headspace. Adjust lids. Do not process or freeze. **Caution: Store in refrigerator and use within 4 weeks.**

Optional: For spiced apple jelly, add 2 sticks of cinnamon and 4 whole cloves to mixture before boiling. Remove both spices before adding the sweetener and food coloring.

REFRIGERATED GRAPE SPREAD (made with gelatin)

2 tbsp unflavored gelatin powder
1 bottle (24 oz) unsweetened grape juice
2 tbsp bottled lemon juice
2 tbsp liquid low-calorie sweetener

Yield: 3 half-pints

Procedure: In a saucepan, soften the gelatin in the grape and lemon juices. Bring to a full rolling boil to dissolve gelatin. Boil 1 minute and remove from heat. Stir in sweetener. Fill jars quickly, leaving 1/4-inch headspace. Adjust lids. Do not process or freeze. **Caution: Store in refrigerator and use within 4 weeks.**

Remaking soft jellies

Measure jelly to be recooked. Work with no more than 4 to 6 cups at a time.

To remake with powdered pectin: For each quart of jelly, mix 1/4 cup sugar, 1/2 cup water, 2 tablespoons bottled lemon juice, and 4 teaspoons powdered pectin. Bring to a boil while stirring. Add jelly and bring to a rolling boil over high heat, stirring constantly. Boil hard 1/2 minute. Remove from heat, quickly skim foam off jelly, and fill sterile jars (see page 1·15), leaving 1/4-inch headspace. Adjust new lids and process.

To remake with liquid pectin: For each quart of jelly, measure 3/4 cup sugar, 2 tablespoons bottled lemon juice, and 2 tablespoons liquid pectin. Bring jelly only to boil over high heat, while stirring. Remove from heat and quickly add the sugar, lemon juice, and pectin. Bring to a full rolling boil, stirring constantly. Boil hard for 1 minute. Quickly skim off foam and fill sterile jars (see page 1·15), leaving 1/4-inch headspace. Adjust new lids and process.

To remake without added pectin: For each quart of jelly, add 2 tablespoons bottled lemon juice. Heat to boiling and boil for 3 to 4 minutes. Use one of the tests described on page 5 to determine jelly doneness. Remove from heat, quickly skim off foam, and fill sterile jars (see page **1·15**), leaving ¼-inch headspace. Adjust new lids and process.

Recommended process time for Remade Soft Jellies in a boiling-water canner

Style of Pack	Jar Size	Process Time at Altitudes of		
		0–1,000 ft	1,001–6,000 ft	Above 6,000 ft
Hot	Half-pints or Pints	5 min	10	15

A CATALOG OF SELECTED
DOVER BOOKS
IN ALL FIELDS OF INTEREST

A CATALOG OF SELECTED DOVER
BOOKS IN ALL FIELDS OF INTEREST

CONCERNING THE SPIRITUAL IN ART, Wassily Kandinsky. Pioneering work by father of abstract art. Thoughts on color theory, nature of art. Analysis of earlier masters. 12 illustrations. 80pp. of text. 5⅜ x 8½.   0-486-23411-8

CELTIC ART: The Methods of Construction, George Bain. Simple geometric techniques for making Celtic interlacements, spirals, Kells-type initials, animals, humans, etc. Over 500 illustrations. 160pp. 9 x 12. (Available in U.S. only.)   0-486-22923-8

AN ATLAS OF ANATOMY FOR ARTISTS, Fritz Schider. Most thorough reference work on art anatomy in the world. Hundreds of illustrations, including selections from works by Vesalius, Leonardo, Goya, Ingres, Michelangelo, others. 593 illustrations. 192pp. 7⅛ x 10¼.   0-486-20241-0

CELTIC HAND STROKE-BY-STROKE (Irish Half-Uncial from "The Book of Kells"): An Arthur Baker Calligraphy Manual, Arthur Baker. Complete guide to creating each letter of the alphabet in distinctive Celtic manner. Covers hand position, strokes, pens, inks, paper, more. Illustrated. 48pp. 8¼ x 11.   0-486-24336-2

EASY ORIGAMI, John Montroll. Charming collection of 32 projects (hat, cup, pelican, piano, swan, many more) specially designed for the novice origami hobbyist. Clearly illustrated easy-to-follow instructions insure that even beginning papercrafters will achieve successful results. 48pp. 8¼ x 11.   0-486-27298-2

BLOOMINGDALE'S ILLUSTRATED 1886 CATALOG: Fashions, Dry Goods and Housewares, Bloomingdale Brothers. Famed merchants' extremely rare catalog depicting about 1,700 products: clothing, housewares, firearms, dry goods, jewelry, more. Invaluable for dating, identifying vintage items. Also, copyright-free graphics for artists, designers. Co-published with Henry Ford Museum & Greenfield Village. 160pp. 8¼ x 11.   0-486-25780-0

THE ART OF WORLDLY WISDOM, Baltasar Gracian. "Think with the few and speak with the many," "Friends are a second existence," and "Be able to forget" are among this 1637 volume's 300 pithy maxims. A perfect source of mental and spiritual refreshment, it can be opened at random and appreciated either in brief or at length. 128pp. 5⅜ x 8½.   0-486-44034-6

JOHNSON'S DICTIONARY: A Modern Selection, Samuel Johnson (E. L. McAdam and George Milne, eds.). This modern version reduces the original 1755 edition's 2,300 pages of definitions and literary examples to a more manageable length, retaining the verbal pleasure and historical curiosity of the original. 480pp. 5³⁄₁₆ x 8¼.   0-486-44089-3

ADVENTURES OF HUCKLEBERRY FINN, Mark Twain, Illustrated by E. W. Kemble. A work of eternal richness and complexity, a source of ongoing critical debate, and a literary landmark, Twain's 1885 masterpiece about a barefoot boy's journey of self-discovery has enthralled readers around the world. This handsome clothbound reproduction of the first edition features all 174 of the original black-and-white illustrations. 368pp. 5⅜ x 8½.   0-486-44322-1

STICKLEY CRAFTSMAN FURNITURE CATALOGS, Gustav Stickley and L. & J. G. Stickley. Beautiful, functional furniture in two authentic catalogs from 1910. 594 illustrations, including 277 photos, show settles, rockers, armchairs, reclining chairs, bookcases, desks, tables. 183pp. 6½ x 9¼.   0-486-23838-5

AMERICAN LOCOMOTIVES IN HISTORIC PHOTOGRAPHS: 1858 to 1949, Ron Ziel (ed.). A rare collection of 126 meticulously detailed official photographs, called "builder portraits," of American locomotives that majestically chronicle the rise of steam locomotive power in America. Introduction. Detailed captions. xi+ 129pp. 9 x 12.   0-486-27393-8

AMERICA'S LIGHTHOUSES: An Illustrated History, Francis Ross Holland, Jr. Delightfully written, profusely illustrated fact-filled survey of over 200 American light-houses since 1716. History, anecdotes, technological advances, more. 240pp. 8 x 10¾.   0-486-25576-X

TOWARDS A NEW ARCHITECTURE, Le Corbusier. Pioneering manifesto by founder of "International School." Technical and aesthetic theories, views of industry, eco-nomics, relation of form to function, "mass-production split" and much more. Profusely illustrated. 320pp. 6⅛ x 9¼. (Available in U.S. only.)   0-486-25023-7

HOW THE OTHER HALF LIVES, Jacob Riis. Famous journalistic record, expos-ing poverty and degradation of New York slums around 1900, by major social reformer. 100 striking and influential photographs. 233pp. 10 x 7⅞.   0-486-22012-5

FRUIT KEY AND TWIG KEY TO TREES AND SHRUBS, William M. Harlow. One of the handiest and most widely used identification aids. Fruit key covers 120 deciduous and evergreen species; twig key 160 deciduous species. Easily used. Over 300 photographs. 126pp. 5⅜ x 8½.   0-486-20511-8

COMMON BIRD SONGS, Dr. Donald J. Borror. Songs of 60 most common U.S. birds: robins, sparrows, cardinals, bluejays, finches, more—arranged in order of increasing complexity. Up to 9 variations of songs of each species.
    Cassette and manual 0-486-99911-4

ORCHIDS AS HOUSE PLANTS, Rebecca Tyson Northen. Grow cattleyas and many other kinds of orchids—in a window, in a case, or under artificial light. 63 illus-trations. 148pp. 5⅜ x 8½.   0-486-23261-1

MONSTER MAZES, Dave Phillips. Masterful mazes at four levels of difficulty. Avoid deadly perils and evil creatures to find magical treasures. Solutions for all 32 exciting illustrated puzzles. 48pp. 8¼ x 11.   0-486-26005-4

MOZART'S DON GIOVANNI (DOVER OPERA LIBRETTO SERIES), Wolfgang Amadeus Mozart. Introduced and translated by Ellen H. Bleiler. Standard Italian libretto, with complete English translation. Convenient and thoroughly portable—an ideal companion for reading along with a recording or the performance itself. Introduction. List of characters. Plot summary. 121pp. 5¼ x 8½. 0-486-24944-1

FRANK LLOYD WRIGHT'S DANA HOUSE, Donald Hoffmann. Pictorial essay of residential masterpiece with over 160 interior and exterior photos, plans, eleva-tions, sketches and studies. 128pp. 9¼ x 10¾.   0-486-29120-0

THE CLARINET AND CLARINET PLAYING, David Pino. Lively, comprehensive work features suggestions about technique, musicianship, and musical interpretation, as well as guidelines for teaching, making your own reeds, and preparing for public performance. Includes an intriguing look at clarinet history. "A godsend," *The Clarinet,* Journal of the International Clarinet Society. Appendixes. 7 illus. 320pp. 5⅜ x 8½. 0-486-40270-3

HOLLYWOOD GLAMOR PORTRAITS, John Kobal (ed.). 145 photos from 1926-49. Harlow, Gable, Bogart, Bacall; 94 stars in all. Full background on photographers, technical aspects. 160pp. 8⅜ x 11¼. 0-486-23352-9

THE RAVEN AND OTHER FAVORITE POEMS, Edgar Allan Poe. Over 40 of the author's most memorable poems: "The Bells," "Ulalume," "Israfel," "To Helen," "The Conqueror Worm," "Eldorado," "Annabel Lee," many more. Alphabetic lists of titles and first lines. 64pp. 5$^{3}/_{16}$ x 8¼. 0-486-26685-0

PERSONAL MEMOIRS OF U. S. GRANT, Ulysses Simpson Grant. Intelligent, deeply moving firsthand account of Civil War campaigns, considered by many the finest military memoirs ever written. Includes letters, historic photographs, maps and more. 528pp. 6⅛ x 9¼. 0-486-28587-1

ANCIENT EGYPTIAN MATERIALS AND INDUSTRIES, A. Lucas and J. Harris. Fascinating, comprehensive, thoroughly documented text describes this ancient civilization's vast resources and the processes that incorporated them in daily life, including the use of animal products, building materials, cosmetics, perfumes and incense, fibers, glazed ware, glass and its manufacture, materials used in the mummification process, and much more. 544pp. 6$^{1}/_{8}$ x 9$^{1}/_{4}$. (Available in U.S. only.) 0-486-40446-3

RUSSIAN STORIES/RUSSKIE RASSKAZY: A Dual-Language Book, edited by Gleb Struve. Twelve tales by such masters as Chekhov, Tolstoy, Dostoevsky, Pushkin, others. Excellent word-for-word English translations on facing pages, plus teaching and study aids, Russian/English vocabulary, biographical/critical introductions, more. 416pp. 5⅜ x 8½. 0-486-26244-8

PHILADELPHIA THEN AND NOW: 60 Sites Photographed in the Past and Present, Kenneth Finkel and Susan Oyama. Rare photographs of City Hall, Logan Square, Independence Hall, Betsy Ross House, other landmarks juxtaposed with contemporary views. Captures changing face of historic city. Introduction. Captions. 128pp. 8¼ x 11. 0-486-25790-8

NORTH AMERICAN INDIAN LIFE: Customs and Traditions of 23 Tribes, Elsie Clews Parsons (ed.). 27 fictionalized essays by noted anthropologists examine religion, customs, government, additional facets of life among the Winnebago, Crow, Zuni, Eskimo, other tribes. 480pp. 6⅛ x 9¼. 0-486-27377-6

TECHNICAL MANUAL AND DICTIONARY OF CLASSICAL BALLET, Gail Grant. Defines, explains, comments on steps, movements, poses and concepts. 15-page pictorial section. Basic book for student, viewer. 127pp. 5⅜ x 8½. 0-486-21843-0

THE MALE AND FEMALE FIGURE IN MOTION: 60 Classic Photographic Sequences, Eadweard Muybridge. 60 true-action photographs of men and women walking, running, climbing, bending, turning, etc., reproduced from rare 19th-century masterpiece. vi + 121pp. 9 x 12. 0-486-24745-7

ANIMALS: 1,419 Copyright-Free Illustrations of Mammals, Birds, Fish, Insects, etc., Jim Harter (ed.). Clear wood engravings present, in extremely lifelike poses, over 1,000 species of animals. One of the most extensive pictorial sourcebooks of its kind. Captions. Index. 284pp. 9 x 12. 0-486-23766-4

1001 QUESTIONS ANSWERED ABOUT THE SEASHORE, N. J. Berrill and Jacquelyn Berrill. Queries answered about dolphins, sea snails, sponges, starfish, fishes, shore birds, many others. Covers appearance, breeding, growth, feeding, much more. 305pp. 5¼ x 8¼. 0-486-23366-9

ATTRACTING BIRDS TO YOUR YARD, William J. Weber. Easy-to-follow guide offers advice on how to attract the greatest diversity of birds: birdhouses, feeders, water and waterers, much more. 96pp. 5³⁄₁₆ x 8¼. 0-486-28927-3

MEDICINAL AND OTHER USES OF NORTH AMERICAN PLANTS: A Historical Survey with Special Reference to the Eastern Indian Tribes, Charlotte Erichsen-Brown. Chronological historical citations document 500 years of usage of plants, trees, shrubs native to eastern Canada, northeastern U.S. Also complete identifying information. 343 illustrations. 544pp. 6½ x 9¼. 0-486-25951-X

STORYBOOK MAZES, Dave Phillips. 23 stories and mazes on two-page spreads: Wizard of Oz, Treasure Island, Robin Hood, etc. Solutions. 64pp. 8¼ x 11.
0-486-23628-5

AMERICAN NEGRO SONGS: 230 Folk Songs and Spirituals, Religious and Secular, John W. Work. This authoritative study traces the African influences of songs sung and played by black Americans at work, in church, and as entertainment. The author discusses the lyric significance of such songs as "Swing Low, Sweet Chariot," "John Henry," and others and offers the words and music for 230 songs. Bibliography. Index of Song Titles. 272pp. 6½ x 9¼. 0-486-40271-1

MOVIE-STAR PORTRAITS OF THE FORTIES, John Kobal (ed.). 163 glamor, studio photos of 106 stars of the 1940s: Rita Hayworth, Ava Gardner, Marlon Brando, Clark Gable, many more. 176pp. 8⅜ x 11¼. 0-486-23546-7

YEKL and THE IMPORTED BRIDEGROOM AND OTHER STORIES OF YIDDISH NEW YORK, Abraham Cahan. Film Hester Street based on *Yekl* (1896). Novel, other stories among first about Jewish immigrants on N.Y.'s East Side. 240pp. 5⅜ x 8½. 0-486-22427-9

SELECTED POEMS, Walt Whitman. Generous sampling from *Leaves of Grass*. Twenty-four poems include "I Hear America Singing," "Song of the Open Road," "I Sing the Body Electric," "When Lilacs Last in the Dooryard Bloom'd," "O Captain! My Captain!"–all reprinted from an authoritative edition. Lists of titles and first lines. 128pp. 5³⁄₁₆ x 8¼. 0-486-26878-0

SONGS OF EXPERIENCE: Facsimile Reproduction with 26 Plates in Full Color, William Blake. 26 full-color plates from a rare 1826 edition. Includes "The Tyger," "London," "Holy Thursday," and other poems. Printed text of poems. 48pp. 5¼ x 7.
0-486-24636-1

THE BEST TALES OF HOFFMANN, E. T. A. Hoffmann. 10 of Hoffmann's most important stories: "Nutcracker and the King of Mice," "The Golden Flowerpot," etc. 458pp. 5⅜ x 8½. 0-486-21793-0

THE BOOK OF TEA, Kakuzo Okakura. Minor classic of the Orient: entertaining, charming explanation, interpretation of traditional Japanese culture in terms of tea ceremony. 94pp. 5⅜ x 8½. 0-486-20070-1

FRENCH STORIES/CONTES FRANÇAIS: A Dual-Language Book, Wallace Fowlie. Ten stories by French masters, Voltaire to Camus: "Micromegas" by Voltaire; "The Atheist's Mass" by Balzac; "Minuet" by de Maupassant; "The Guest" by Camus, six more. Excellent English translations on facing pages. Also French-English vocabulary list, exercises, more. 352pp. 5⅜ x 8½. 0-486-26443-2

CHICAGO AT THE TURN OF THE CENTURY IN PHOTOGRAPHS: 122 Historic Views from the Collections of the Chicago Historical Society, Larry A. Viskochil. Rare large-format prints offer detailed views of City Hall, State Street, the Loop, Hull House, Union Station, many other landmarks, circa 1904-1913. Introduction. Captions. Maps. 144pp. 9⅜ x 12¼. 0-486-24656-6

OLD BROOKLYN IN EARLY PHOTOGRAPHS, 1865-1929, William Lee Younger. Luna Park, Gravesend race track, construction of Grand Army Plaza, moving of Hotel Brighton, etc. 157 previously unpublished photographs. 165pp. 8⅞ x 11¾. 0-486-23587-4

THE MYTHS OF THE NORTH AMERICAN INDIANS, Lewis Spence. Rich anthology of the myths and legends of the Algonquins, Iroquois, Pawnees and Sioux, prefaced by an extensive historical and ethnological commentary. 36 illustrations. 480pp. 5⅜ x 8½. 0-486-25967-6

AN ENCYCLOPEDIA OF BATTLES: Accounts of Over 1,560 Battles from 1479 B.C. to the Present, David Eggenberger. Essential details of every major battle in recorded history from the first battle of Megiddo in 1479 B.C. to Grenada in 1984. List of Battle Maps. New Appendix covering the years 1967-1984. Index. 99 illustrations. 544pp. 6½ x 9¼. 0-486-24913-1

SAILING ALONE AROUND THE WORLD, Captain Joshua Slocum. First man to sail around the world, alone, in small boat. One of great feats of seamanship told in delightful manner. 67 illustrations. 294pp. 5⅜ x 8½. 0-486-20326-3

ANARCHISM AND OTHER ESSAYS, Emma Goldman. Powerful, penetrating, prophetic essays on direct action, role of minorities, prison reform, puritan hypocrisy, violence, etc. 271pp. 5⅜ x 8½. 0-486-22484-8

MYTHS OF THE HINDUS AND BUDDHISTS, Ananda K. Coomaraswamy and Sister Nivedita. Great stories of the epics; deeds of Krishna, Shiva, taken from puranas, Vedas, folk tales; etc. 32 illustrations. 400pp. 5⅜ x 8½. 0-486-21759-0

MY BONDAGE AND MY FREEDOM, Frederick Douglass. Born a slave, Douglass became outspoken force in antislavery movement. The best of Douglass' autobiographies. Graphic description of slave life. 464pp. 5⅜ x 8½. 0-486-22457-0

FOLLOWING THE EQUATOR: A Journey Around the World, Mark Twain. Fascinating humorous account of 1897 voyage to Hawaii, Australia, India, New Zealand, etc. Ironic, bemused reports on peoples, customs, climate, flora and fauna, politics, much more. 197 illustrations. 720pp. 5⅜ x 8½. 0-486-26113-1

THE PEOPLE CALLED SHAKERS, Edward D. Andrews. Definitive study of Shakers: origins, beliefs, practices, dances, social organization, furniture and crafts, etc. 33 illustrations. 351pp. 5⅜ x 8½. 0-486-21081-2

THE MYTHS OF GREECE AND ROME, H. A. Guerber. A classic of mythology, generously illustrated, long prized for its simple, graphic, accurate retelling of the principal myths of Greece and Rome, and for its commentary on their origins and significance. With 64 illustrations by Michelangelo, Raphael, Titian, Rubens, Canova, Bernini and others. 480pp. 5⅜ x 8½. 0-486-27584-1

PSYCHOLOGY OF MUSIC, Carl E. Seashore. Classic work discusses music as a medium from psychological viewpoint. Clear treatment of physical acoustics, auditory apparatus, sound perception, development of musical skills, nature of musical feeling, host of other topics. 88 figures. 408pp. 5⅜ x 8½.　　0-486-21851-1

LIFE IN ANCIENT EGYPT, Adolf Erman. Fullest, most thorough, detailed older account with much not in more recent books, domestic life, religion, magic, medicine, commerce, much more. Many illustrations reproduce tomb paintings, carvings, hieroglyphs, etc. 597pp. 5⅜ x 8½.　　0-486-22632-8

SUNDIALS, Their Theory and Construction, Albert Waugh. Far and away the best, most thorough coverage of ideas, mathematics concerned, types, construction, adjusting anywhere. Simple, nontechnical treatment allows even children to build several of these dials. Over 100 illustrations. 230pp. 5⅜ x 8½.　　0-486-22947-5

THEORETICAL HYDRODYNAMICS, L. M. Milne-Thomson. Classic exposition of the mathematical theory of fluid motion, applicable to both hydrodynamics and aerodynamics. Over 600 exercises. 768pp. 6⅛ x 9¼.　　0-486-68970-0

OLD-TIME VIGNETTES IN FULL COLOR, Carol Belanger Grafton (ed.). Over 390 charming, often sentimental illustrations, selected from archives of Victorian graphics—pretty women posing, children playing, food, flowers, kittens and puppies, smiling cherubs, birds and butterflies, much more. All copyright-free. 48pp. 9¼ x 12¼.
0-486-27269-9

PERSPECTIVE FOR ARTISTS, Rex Vicat Cole. Depth, perspective of sky and sea, shadows, much more, not usually covered. 391 diagrams, 81 reproductions of drawings and paintings. 279pp. 5⅜ x 8½.　　0-486-22487-2

DRAWING THE LIVING FIGURE, Joseph Sheppard. Innovative approach to artistic anatomy focuses on specifics of surface anatomy, rather than muscles and bones. Over 170 drawings of live models in front, back and side views, and in widely varying poses. Accompanying diagrams. 177 illustrations. Introduction. Index. 144pp. 8⅜ x11¼.　　0-486-26723-7

GOTHIC AND OLD ENGLISH ALPHABETS: 100 Complete Fonts, Dan X. Solo. Add power, elegance to posters, signs, other graphics with 100 stunning copyright-free alphabets: Blackstone, Dolbey, Germania, 97 more—including many lower-case, numerals, punctuation marks. 104pp. 8⅛ x 11.　　0-486-24695-7

THE BOOK OF WOOD CARVING, Charles Marshall Sayers. Finest book for beginners discusses fundamentals and offers 34 designs. "Absolutely first rate . . . well thought out and well executed."–E. J. Tangerman. 118pp. 7¾ x 10⅝.　0-486-23654-4

ILLUSTRATED CATALOG OF CIVIL WAR MILITARY GOODS: Union Army Weapons, Insignia, Uniform Accessories, and Other Equipment, Schuyler, Hartley, and Graham. Rare, profusely illustrated 1846 catalog includes Union Army uniform and dress regulations, arms and ammunition, coats, insignia, flags, swords, rifles, etc. 226 illustrations. 160pp. 9 x 12.　　0-486-24939-5

WOMEN'S FASHIONS OF THE EARLY 1900s: An Unabridged Republication of "New York Fashions, 1909," National Cloak & Suit Co. Rare catalog of mail-order fashions documents women's and children's clothing styles shortly after the turn of the century. Captions offer full descriptions, prices. Invaluable resource for fashion, costume historians. Approximately 725 illustrations. 128pp. 8⅜ x 11¼.
0-486-27276-1

HOW TO DO BEADWORK, Mary White. Fundamental book on craft from simple projects to five-bead chains and woven works. 106 illustrations. 142pp. 5⅜ x 8.
0-486-20697-1

THE 1912 AND 1915 GUSTAV STICKLEY FURNITURE CATALOGS, Gustav Stickley. With over 200 detailed illustrations and descriptions, these two catalogs are essential reading and reference materials and identification guides for Stickley furniture. Captions cite materials, dimensions and prices. 112pp. 6½ x 9¼. 0-486-26676-1

EARLY AMERICAN LOCOMOTIVES, John H. White, Jr. Finest locomotive engravings from early 19th century: historical (1804–74), main-line (after 1870), special, foreign, etc. 147 plates. 142pp. 11⅜ x 8¼. 0-486-22772-3

LITTLE BOOK OF EARLY AMERICAN CRAFTS AND TRADES, Peter Stockham (ed.). 1807 children's book explains crafts and trades: baker, hatter, cooper, potter, and many others. 23 copperplate illustrations. 140pp. 4⁵/₈ x 6.
0-486-23336-7

VICTORIAN FASHIONS AND COSTUMES FROM HARPER'S BAZAR, 1867–1898, Stella Blum (ed.). Day costumes, evening wear, sports clothes, shoes, hats, other accessories in over 1,000 detailed engravings. 320pp. 9⅜ x 12¼.
0-486-22990-4

THE LONG ISLAND RAIL ROAD IN EARLY PHOTOGRAPHS, Ron Ziel. Over 220 rare photos, informative text document origin (1844) and development of rail service on Long Island. Vintage views of early trains, locomotives, stations, passengers, crews, much more. Captions. 8⅞ x 11¾. 0-486-26301-0

VOYAGE OF THE LIBERDADE, Joshua Slocum. Great 19th-century mariner's thrilling, first-hand account of the wreck of his ship off South America, the 35-foot boat he built from the wreckage, and its remarkable voyage home. 128pp. 5⅜ x 8½.
0-486-40022-0

TEN BOOKS ON ARCHITECTURE, Vitruvius. The most important book ever written on architecture. Early Roman aesthetics, technology, classical orders, site selection, all other aspects. Morgan translation. 331pp. 5⅜ x 8½. 0-486-20645-9

THE HUMAN FIGURE IN MOTION, Eadweard Muybridge. More than 4,500 stopped-action photos, in action series, showing undraped men, women, children jumping, lying down, throwing, sitting, wrestling, carrying, etc. 390pp. 7⅞ x 10⅝.
0-486-20204-6 Clothbd.

TREES OF THE EASTERN AND CENTRAL UNITED STATES AND CANADA, William M. Harlow. Best one-volume guide to 140 trees. Full descriptions, woodlore, range, etc. Over 600 illustrations. Handy size. 288pp. 4½ x 6⅜. 0-486-20395-6

GROWING AND USING HERBS AND SPICES, Milo Miloradovich. Versatile handbook provides all the information needed for cultivation and use of all the herbs and spices available in North America. 4 illustrations. Index. Glossary. 236pp. 5⅜ x 8½.
0-486-25058-X

BIG BOOK OF MAZES AND LABYRINTHS, Walter Shepherd. 50 mazes and labyrinths in all–classical, solid, ripple, and more–in one great volume. Perfect inexpensive puzzler for clever youngsters. Full solutions. 112pp. 8⅛ x 11. 0-486-22951-3

PIANO TUNING, J. Cree Fischer. Clearest, best book for beginner, amateur. Simple repairs, raising dropped notes, tuning by easy method of flattened fifths. No previous skills needed. 4 illustrations. 201pp. 5⅜ x 8½. 0-486-23267-0

HINTS TO SINGERS, Lillian Nordica. Selecting the right teacher, developing confidence, overcoming stage fright, and many other important skills receive thoughtful discussion in this indispensible guide, written by a world-famous diva of four decades' experience. 96pp. 5⅜ x 8½. 0-486-40094-8

THE COMPLETE NONSENSE OF EDWARD LEAR, Edward Lear. All nonsense limericks, zany alphabets, Owl and Pussycat, songs, nonsense botany, etc., illustrated by Lear. Total of 320pp. 5⅜ x 8½. (Available in U.S. only.) 0-486-20167-8

VICTORIAN PARLOUR POETRY: An Annotated Anthology, Michael R. Turner. 117 gems by Longfellow, Tennyson, Browning, many lesser-known poets. "The Village Blacksmith," "Curfew Must Not Ring Tonight," "Only a Baby Small," dozens more, often difficult to find elsewhere. Index of poets, titles, first lines. xxiii + 325pp. 5⅝ x 8¼. 0-486-27044-0

DUBLINERS, James Joyce. Fifteen stories offer vivid, tightly focused observations of the lives of Dublin's poorer classes. At least one, "The Dead," is considered a masterpiece. Reprinted complete and unabridged from standard edition. 160pp. 5³⁄₁₆ x 8¼. 0-486-26870-5

GREAT WEIRD TALES: 14 Stories by Lovecraft, Blackwood, Machen and Others, S. T. Joshi (ed.). 14 spellbinding tales, including "The Sin Eater," by Fiona McLeod, "The Eye Above the Mantel," by Frank Belknap Long, as well as renowned works by R. H. Barlow, Lord Dunsany, Arthur Machen, W. C. Morrow and eight other masters of the genre. 256pp. 5⅜ x 8½. (Available in U.S. only.) 0-486-40436-6

THE BOOK OF THE SACRED MAGIC OF ABRAMELIN THE MAGE, translated by S. MacGregor Mathers. Medieval manuscript of ceremonial magic. Basic document in Aleister Crowley, Golden Dawn groups. 268pp. 5⅜ x 8½. 0-486-23211-5

THE BATTLES THAT CHANGED HISTORY, Fletcher Pratt. Eminent historian profiles 16 crucial conflicts, ancient to modern, that changed the course of civilization. 352pp. 5⅜ x 8½. 0-486-41129-X

NEW RUSSIAN-ENGLISH AND ENGLISH-RUSSIAN DICTIONARY, M. A. O'Brien. This is a remarkably handy Russian dictionary, containing a surprising amount of information, including over 70,000 entries. 366pp. 4½ x 6⅛. 0-486-20208-9

NEW YORK IN THE FORTIES, Andreas Feininger. 162 brilliant photographs by the well-known photographer, formerly with *Life* magazine. Commuters, shoppers, Times Square at night, much else from city at its peak. Captions by John von Hartz. 181pp. 9¼ x 10¾. 0-486-23585-8

INDIAN SIGN LANGUAGE, William Tomkins. Over 525 signs developed by Sioux and other tribes. Written instructions and diagrams. Also 290 pictographs. 111pp. 6⅛ x 9¼. 0-486-22029-X

ANATOMY: A Complete Guide for Artists, Joseph Sheppard. A master of figure drawing shows artists how to render human anatomy convincingly. Over 460 illustrations. 224pp. 8⅜ x 11¼. 0-486-27279-6

MEDIEVAL CALLIGRAPHY: Its History and Technique, Marc Drogin. Spirited history, comprehensive instruction manual covers 13 styles (ca. 4th century through 15th). Excellent photographs; directions for duplicating medieval techniques with modern tools. 224pp. 8⅜ x 11¼. 0-486-26142-5

DRIED FLOWERS: How to Prepare Them, Sarah Whitlock and Martha Rankin. Complete instructions on how to use silica gel, meal and borax, perlite aggregate, sand and borax, glycerine and water to create attractive permanent flower arrangements. 12 illustrations. 32pp. 5⅜ x 8½. 0-486-21802-3

EASY-TO-MAKE BIRD FEEDERS FOR WOODWORKERS, Scott D. Campbell. Detailed, simple-to-use guide for designing, constructing, caring for and using feeders. Text, illustrations for 12 classic and contemporary designs. 96pp. 5⅜ x 8½. 0-486-25847-5

THE COMPLETE BOOK OF BIRDHOUSE CONSTRUCTION FOR WOODWORKERS, Scott D. Campbell. Detailed instructions, illustrations, tables. Also data on bird habitat and instinct patterns. Bibliography. 3 tables. 63 illustrations in 15 figures. 48pp. 5¼ x 8½. 0-486-24407-5

SCOTTISH WONDER TALES FROM MYTH AND LEGEND, Donald A. Mackenzie. 16 lively tales tell of giants rumbling down mountainsides, of a magic wand that turns stone pillars into warriors, of gods and goddesses, evil hags, powerful forces and more. 240pp. 5⅜ x 8½. 0-486-29677-6

THE HISTORY OF UNDERCLOTHES, C. Willett Cunnington and Phyllis Cunnington. Fascinating, well-documented survey covering six centuries of English undergarments, enhanced with over 100 illustrations: 12th-century laced-up bodice, footed long drawers (1795), 19th-century bustles, 19th-century corsets for men, Victorian "bust improvers," much more. 272pp. 5⅜ x 8¼. 0-486-27124-2

ARTS AND CRAFTS FURNITURE: The Complete Brooks Catalog of 1912, Brooks Manufacturing Co. Photos and detailed descriptions of more than 150 now very collectible furniture designs from the Arts and Crafts movement depict davenports, settees, buffets, desks, tables, chairs, bedsteads, dressers and more, all built of solid, quarter-sawed oak. Invaluable for students and enthusiasts of antiques, Americana and the decorative arts. 80pp. 6½ x 9¼. 0-486-27471-3

WILBUR AND ORVILLE: A Biography of the Wright Brothers, Fred Howard. Definitive, crisply written study tells the full story of the brothers' lives and work. A vividly written biography, unparalleled in scope and color, that also captures the spirit of an extraordinary era. 560pp. 6⅛ x 9¼. 0-486-40297-5

THE ARTS OF THE SAILOR: Knotting, Splicing and Ropework, Hervey Garrett Smith. Indispensable shipboard reference covers tools, basic knots and useful hitches; handsewing and canvas work, more. Over 100 illustrations. Delightful reading for sea lovers. 256pp. 5⅜ x 8½. 0-486-26440-8

FRANK LLOYD WRIGHT'S FALLINGWATER: The House and Its History, Second, Revised Edition, Donald Hoffmann. A total revision–both in text and illustrations–of the standard document on Fallingwater, the boldest, most personal architectural statement of Wright's mature years, updated with valuable new material from the recently opened Frank Lloyd Wright Archives. "Fascinating"–*The New York Times*. 116 illustrations. 128pp. 9¼ x 10¾. 0-486-27430-6

PHOTOGRAPHIC SKETCHBOOK OF THE CIVIL WAR, Alexander Gardner. 100 photos taken on field during the Civil War. Famous shots of Manassas Harper's Ferry, Lincoln, Richmond, slave pens, etc. 244pp. 10⅝ x 8¼. 0-486-22731-6

FIVE ACRES AND INDEPENDENCE, Maurice G. Kains. Great back-to-the-land classic explains basics of self-sufficient farming. The one book to get. 95 illustrations. 397pp. 5⅜ x 8½. 0-486-20974-1

CATALOG OF DOVER BOOKS

A MODERN HERBAL, Margaret Grieve. Much the fullest, most exact, most useful compilation of herbal material. Gigantic alphabetical encyclopedia, from aconite to zedoary, gives botanical information, medical properties, folklore, economic uses, much else. Indispensable to serious reader. 161 illustrations. 888pp. 6½ x 9¼. 2-vol. set. (Available in U.S. only.)   Vol. I: 0-486-22798-7   Vol. II: 0-486-22799-5

HIDDEN TREASURE MAZE BOOK, Dave Phillips. Solve 34 challenging mazes accompanied by heroic tales of adventure. Evil dragons, people-eating plants, blood-thirsty giants, many more dangerous adversaries lurk at every twist and turn. 34 mazes, stories, solutions. 48pp. 8¼ x 11.   0-486-24566-7

LETTERS OF W. A. MOZART, Wolfgang A. Mozart. Remarkable letters show bawdy wit, humor, imagination, musical insights, contemporary musical world; includes some letters from Leopold Mozart. 276pp. 5⅜ x 8½.   0-486-22859-2

BASIC PRINCIPLES OF CLASSICAL BALLET, Agrippina Vaganova. Great Russian theoretician, teacher explains methods for teaching classical ballet. 118 illustrations. 175pp. 5⅜ x 8½.   0-486-22036-2

THE JUMPING FROG, Mark Twain. Revenge edition. The original story of The Celebrated Jumping Frog of Calaveras County, a hapless French translation, and Twain's hilarious "retranslation" from the French. 12 illustrations. 66pp. 5⅜ x 8½.   0-486-22686-7

BEST REMEMBERED POEMS, Martin Gardner (ed.). The 126 poems in this superb collection of 19th- and 20th-century British and American verse range from Shelley's "To a Skylark" to the impassioned "Renascence" of Edna St. Vincent Millay and to Edward Lear's whimsical "The Owl and the Pussycat." 224pp. 5⅜ x 8½.   0-486-27165-X

COMPLETE SONNETS, William Shakespeare. Over 150 exquisite poems deal with love, friendship, the tyranny of time, beauty's evanescence, death and other themes in language of remarkable power, precision and beauty. Glossary of archaic terms. 80pp. 5³⁄₁₆ x 8¼.   0-486-26686-9

HISTORIC HOMES OF THE AMERICAN PRESIDENTS, Second, Revised Edition, Irvin Haas. A traveler's guide to American Presidential homes, most open to the public, depicting and describing homes occupied by every American President from George Washington to George Bush. With visiting hours, admission charges, travel routes. 175 photographs. Index. 160pp. 8¼ x 11.   0-486-26751-2

THE WIT AND HUMOR OF OSCAR WILDE, Alvin Redman (ed.). More than 1,000 ripostes, paradoxes, wisecracks: Work is the curse of the drinking classes; I can resist everything except temptation; etc. 258pp. 5⅜ x 8½.   0-486-20602-5

SHAKESPEARE LEXICON AND QUOTATION DICTIONARY, Alexander Schmidt. Full definitions, locations, shades of meaning in every word in plays and poems. More than 50,000 exact quotations. 1,485pp. 6½ x 9¼. 2-vol. set.
Vol. 1: 0-486-22726-X   Vol. 2: 0-486-22727-8

SELECTED POEMS, Emily Dickinson. Over 100 best-known, best-loved poems by one of America's foremost poets, reprinted from authoritative early editions. No comparable edition at this price. Index of first lines. 64pp. 5³⁄₁₆ x 8¼. 0-486-26466-1

THE INSIDIOUS DR. FU-MANCHU, Sax Rohmer. The first of the popular mystery series introduces a pair of English detectives to their archnemesis, the diabolical Dr. Fu-Manchu. Flavorful atmosphere, fast-paced action, and colorful characters enliven this classic of the genre. 208pp. 5³⁄₁₆ x 8¼.   0-486-29898-1

THE MALLEUS MALEFICARUM OF KRAMER AND SPRENGER, translated by Montague Summers. Full text of most important witchhunter's "bible," used by both Catholics and Protestants. 278pp. 6⅝ x 10. 0-486-22802-9

SPANISH STORIES/CUENTOS ESPAÑOLES: A Dual-Language Book, Angel Flores (ed.). Unique format offers 13 great stories in Spanish by Cervantes, Borges, others. Faithful English translations on facing pages. 352pp. 5⅜ x 8½.

0-486-25399-6

GARDEN CITY, LONG ISLAND, IN EARLY PHOTOGRAPHS, 1869–1919, Mildred H. Smith. Handsome treasury of 118 vintage pictures, accompanied by carefully researched captions, document the Garden City Hotel fire (1899), the Vanderbilt Cup Race (1908), the first airmail flight departing from the Nassau Boulevard Aerodrome (1911), and much more. 96pp. 8⅞ x 11¾. 0-486-40669-5

OLD QUEENS, N.Y., IN EARLY PHOTOGRAPHS, Vincent F. Seyfried and William Asadorian. Over 160 rare photographs of Maspeth, Jamaica, Jackson Heights, and other areas. Vintage views of DeWitt Clinton mansion, 1939 World's Fair and more. Captions. 192pp. 8⅞ x 11. 0-486-26358-4

CAPTURED BY THE INDIANS: 15 Firsthand Accounts, 1750-1870, Frederick Drimmer. Astounding true historical accounts of grisly torture, bloody conflicts, relentless pursuits, miraculous escapes and more, by people who lived to tell the tale. 384pp. 5⅜ x 8½. 0-486-24901-8

THE WORLD'S GREAT SPEECHES (Fourth Enlarged Edition), Lewis Copeland, Lawrence W. Lamm, and Stephen J. McKenna. Nearly 300 speeches provide public speakers with a wealth of updated quotes and inspiration–from Pericles' funeral oration and William Jennings Bryan's "Cross of Gold Speech" to Malcolm X's powerful words on the Black Revolution and Earl of Spenser's tribute to his sister, Diana, Princess of Wales. 944pp. 5⅜ x 8⅜. 0-486-40903-1

THE BOOK OF THE SWORD, Sir Richard F. Burton. Great Victorian scholar/adventurer's eloquent, erudite history of the "queen of weapons"–from prehistory to early Roman Empire. Evolution and development of early swords, variations (sabre, broadsword, cutlass, scimitar, etc.), much more. 336pp. 6⅛ x 9¼.

0-486-25434-8

AUTOBIOGRAPHY: The Story of My Experiments with Truth, Mohandas K. Gandhi. Boyhood, legal studies, purification, the growth of the Satyagraha (nonviolent protest) movement. Critical, inspiring work of the man responsible for the freedom of India. 480pp. 5⅜ x 8½. (Available in U.S. only.) 0-486-24593-4

CELTIC MYTHS AND LEGENDS, T. W. Rolleston. Masterful retelling of Irish and Welsh stories and tales. Cuchulain, King Arthur, Deirdre, the Grail, many more. First paperback edition. 58 full-page illustrations. 512pp. 5⅜ x 8½. 0-486-26507-2

THE PRINCIPLES OF PSYCHOLOGY, William James. Famous long course complete, unabridged. Stream of thought, time perception, memory, experimental methods; great work decades ahead of its time. 94 figures. 1,391pp. 5⅜ x 8½. 2-vol. set.
Vol. I: 0-486-20381-6   Vol. II: 0-486-20382-4

THE WORLD AS WILL AND REPRESENTATION, Arthur Schopenhauer. Definitive English translation of Schopenhauer's life work, correcting more than 1,000 errors, omissions in earlier translations. Translated by E. F. J. Payne. Total of 1,269pp. 5⅜ x 8½. 2-vol. set.   Vol. 1: 0-486-21761-2   Vol. 2: 0-486-21762-0

MAGIC AND MYSTERY IN TIBET, Madame Alexandra David-Neel. Experiences among lamas, magicians, sages, sorcerers, Bonpa wizards. A true psychic discovery. 32 illustrations. 321pp. 5⅜ x 8½. (Available in U.S. only.)   0-486-22682-4

THE EGYPTIAN BOOK OF THE DEAD, E. A. Wallis Budge. Complete reproduction of Ani's papyrus, finest ever found. Full hieroglyphic text, interlinear transliteration, word-for-word translation, smooth translation. 533pp. 6½ x 9¼.
0-486-21866-X

HISTORIC COSTUME IN PICTURES, Braun & Schneider. Over 1,450 costumed figures in clearly detailed engravings–from dawn of civilization to end of 19th century. Captions. Many folk costumes. 256pp. 8⅜ x 11¾.   0-486-23150-X

MATHEMATICS FOR THE NONMATHEMATICIAN, Morris Kline. Detailed, college-level treatment of mathematics in cultural and historical context, with numerous exercises. Recommended Reading Lists. Tables. Numerous figures. 641pp. 5⅜ x 8½.
0-486-24823-2

PROBABILISTIC METHODS IN THE THEORY OF STRUCTURES, Isaac Elishakoff. Well-written introduction covers the elements of the theory of probability from two or more random variables, the reliability of such multivariable structures, the theory of random function, Monte Carlo methods of treating problems incapable of exact solution, and more. Examples. 502pp. 5⅜ x 8½.   0-486-40691-1

THE RIME OF THE ANCIENT MARINER, Gustave Doré, S. T. Coleridge. Doré's finest work; 34 plates capture moods, subtleties of poem. Flawless full-size reproductions printed on facing pages with authoritative text of poem. "Beautiful. Simply beautiful."–*Publisher's Weekly.* 77pp. 9¼ x 12.   0-486-22305-1

SCULPTURE: Principles and Practice, Louis Slobodkin. Step-by-step approach to clay, plaster, metals, stone; classical and modern. 253 drawings, photos. 255pp. 8⅛ x 11.
0-486-22960-2

THE INFLUENCE OF SEA POWER UPON HISTORY, 1660–1783, A. T. Mahan. Influential classic of naval history and tactics still used as text in war colleges. First paperback edition. 4 maps. 24 battle plans. 640pp. 5⅜ x 8½.   0-486-25509-3

THE STORY OF THE TITANIC AS TOLD BY ITS SURVIVORS, Jack Winocour (ed.). What it was really like. Panic, despair, shocking inefficiency, and a little heroism. More thrilling than any fictional account. 26 illustrations. 320pp. 5⅜ x 8½.
0-486-20610-6

ONE TWO THREE . . . INFINITY: Facts and Speculations of Science, George Gamow. Great physicist's fascinating, readable overview of contemporary science: number theory, relativity, fourth dimension, entropy, genes, atomic structure, much more. 128 illustrations. Index. 352pp. 5⅜ x 8½.   0-486-25664-2

DALÍ ON MODERN ART: The Cuckolds of Antiquated Modern Art, Salvador Dalí. Influential painter skewers modern art and its practitioners. Outrageous evaluations of Picasso, Cézanne, Turner, more. 15 renderings of paintings discussed. 44 calligraphic decorations by Dalí. 96pp. 5⅜ x 8½. (Available in U.S. only.)   0-486-29220-7

ANTIQUE PLAYING CARDS: A Pictorial History, Henry René D'Allemagne. Over 900 elaborate, decorative images from rare playing cards (14th–20th centuries): Bacchus, death, dancing dogs, hunting scenes, royal coats of arms, players cheating, much more. 96pp. 9¼ x 12¼.   0-486-29265-7

MAKING FURNITURE MASTERPIECES: 30 Projects with Measured Drawings, Franklin H. Gottshall. Step-by-step instructions, illustrations for constructing handsome, useful pieces, among them a Sheraton desk, Chippendale chair, Spanish desk, Queen Anne table and a William and Mary dressing mirror. 224pp. 8⅛ x 11¼. 0-486-29338-6

NORTH AMERICAN INDIAN DESIGNS FOR ARTISTS AND CRAFTSPEOPLE, Eva Wilson. Over 360 authentic copyright-free designs adapted from Navajo blankets, Hopi pottery, Sioux buffalo hides, more. Geometrics, symbolic figures, plant and animal motifs, etc. 128pp. 8⅜ x 11. (Not for sale in the United Kingdom.) 0-486-25341-4

THE FOSSIL BOOK: A Record of Prehistoric Life, Patricia V. Rich et al. Profusely illustrated definitive guide covers everything from single-celled organisms and dinosaurs to birds and mammals and the interplay between climate and man. Over 1,500 illustrations. 760pp. 7½ x 10⅛. 0-486-29371-8

VICTORIAN ARCHITECTURAL DETAILS: Designs for Over 700 Stairs, Mantels, Doors, Windows, Cornices, Porches, and Other Decorative Elements, A. J. Bicknell & Company. Everything from dormer windows and piazzas to balconies and gable ornaments. Also includes elevations and floor plans for handsome, private residences and commercial structures. 80pp. 9⅜ x 12¼. 0-486-44015-X

WESTERN ISLAMIC ARCHITECTURE: A Concise Introduction, John D. Hoag. Profusely illustrated critical appraisal compares and contrasts Islamic mosques and palaces–from Spain and Egypt to other areas in the Middle East. 139 illustrations. 128pp. 6 x 9. 0-486-43760-4

CHINESE ARCHITECTURE: A Pictorial History, Liang Ssu-ch'eng. More than 240 rare photographs and drawings depict temples, pagodas, tombs, bridges, and imperial palaces comprising much of China's architectural heritage. 152 halftones, 94 diagrams. 232pp. 10¾ x 9⅞. 0-486-43999-2

THE RENAISSANCE: Studies in Art and Poetry, Walter Pater. One of the most talked-about books of the 19th century, *The Renaissance* combines scholarship and philosophy in an innovative work of cultural criticism that examines the achievements of Botticelli, Leonardo, Michelangelo, and other artists. "The holy writ of beauty."–Oscar Wilde. 160pp. 5⅜ x 8½. 0-486-44025-7

A TREATISE ON PAINTING, Leonardo da Vinci. The great Renaissance artist's practical advice on drawing and painting techniques covers anatomy, perspective, composition, light and shadow, and color. A classic of art instruction, it features 48 drawings by Nicholas Poussin and Leon Battista Alberti. 192pp. 5⅜ x 8½. 0-486-44155-5

THE MIND OF LEONARDO DA VINCI, Edward McCurdy. More than just a biography, this classic study by a distinguished historian draws upon Leonardo's extensive writings to offer numerous demonstrations of the Renaissance master's achievements, not only in sculpture and painting, but also in music, engineering, and even experimental aviation. 384pp. 5⅜ x 8½. 0-486-44142-3

WASHINGTON IRVING'S RIP VAN WINKLE, Illustrated by Arthur Rackham. Lovely prints that established artist as a leading illustrator of the time and forever etched into the popular imagination a classic of Catskill lore. 51 full-color plates. 80pp. 8⅜ x 11. 0-486-44242-X

HENSCHE ON PAINTING, John W. Robichaux. Basic painting philosophy and methodology of a great teacher, as expounded in his famous classes and workshops on Cape Cod. 7 illustrations in color on covers. 80pp. 5⅜ x 8½. 0-486-43728-0

CATALOG OF DOVER BOOKS

LIGHT AND SHADE: A Classic Approach to Three-Dimensional Drawing, Mrs. Mary P. Merrifield. Handy reference clearly demonstrates principles of light and shade by revealing effects of common daylight, sunshine, and candle or artificial light on geometrical solids. 13 plates. 64pp. 5⅜ x 8½. 0-486-44143-1

ASTROLOGY AND ASTRONOMY: A Pictorial Archive of Signs and Symbols, Ernst and Johanna Lehner. Treasure trove of stories, lore, and myth, accompanied by more than 300 rare illustrations of planets, the Milky Way, signs of the zodiac, comets, meteors, and other astronomical phenomena. 192pp. 8⅜ x 11. 0-486-43981-X

JEWELRY MAKING: Techniques for Metal, Tim McCreight. Easy-to-follow instructions and carefully executed illustrations describe tools and techniques, use of gems and enamels, wire inlay, casting, and other topics. 72 line illustrations and diagrams. 176pp. 8¼ x 10⅞. 0-486-44043-5

MAKING BIRDHOUSES: Easy and Advanced Projects, Gladstone Califf. Easy-to-follow instructions include diagrams for everything from a one-room house for bluebirds to a forty-two-room structure for purple martins. 56 plates; 4 figures. 80pp. 8¾ x 6⅜. 0-486-44183-0

LITTLE BOOK OF LOG CABINS: How to Build and Furnish Them, William S. Wicks. Handy how-to manual, with instructions and illustrations for building cabins in the Adirondack style, fireplaces, stairways, furniture, beamed ceilings, and more. 102 line drawings. 96pp. 8¾ x 6⅜. 0-486-44259-4

THE SEASONS OF AMERICA PAST, Eric Sloane. From "sugaring time" and strawberry picking to Indian summer and fall harvest, a whole year's activities described in charming prose and enhanced with 79 of the author's own illustrations. 160pp. 8¼ x 11. 0-486-44220-9

THE METROPOLIS OF TOMORROW, Hugh Ferriss. Generous, prophetic vision of the metropolis of the future, as perceived in 1929. Powerful illustrations of towering structures, wide avenues, and rooftop parks–all features in many of today's modern cities. 59 illustrations. 144pp. 8¼ x 11. 0-486-43727-2

THE PATH TO ROME, Hilaire Belloc. This 1902 memoir abounds in lively vignettes from a vanished time, recounting a pilgrimage on foot across the Alps and Apennines in order to "see all Europe which the Christian Faith has saved." 77 of the author's original line drawings complement his sparkling prose. 272pp. 5⅜ x 8½. 0-486-44001-X

THE HISTORY OF RASSELAS: Prince of Abissinia, Samuel Johnson. Distinguished English writer attacks eighteenth-century optimism and man's unrealistic estimates of what life has to offer. 112pp. 5⅜ x 8½. 0-486-44094-X

A VOYAGE TO ARCTURUS, David Lindsay. A brilliant flight of pure fancy, where wild creatures crowd the fantastic landscape and demented torturers dominate victims with their bizarre mental powers. 272pp. 5⅜ x 8½. 0-486-44198-9

Paperbound unless otherwise indicated. Available at your book dealer, online at **www.doverpublications.com**, or by writing to Dept. GI, Dover Publications, Inc., 31 East 2nd Street, Mineola, NY 11501. For current price information or for free catalogs (please indicate field of interest), write to Dover Publications or log on to **www.doverpublications.com** and see every Dover book in print. Dover publishes more than 500 books each year on science, elementary and advanced mathematics, biology, music, art, literary history, social sciences, and other areas.